Essentials

AutoCAD®
Raster Design 2017 (R1)

November 2016

AUTODESK.
Authorized Publisher

Contents

Introduction

Welcome to the *AutoCAD Raster Design 2017 (R1): Essentials* training courseware for use in Authorized Training Center (ATC) locations, corporate training settings, and other classroom settings.

Although this courseware is designed for instructor-led courses, you can also use it for self-paced learning. The courseware encourages self-learning through the use of the AutoCAD® Raster Design 2017 Help system.

This courseware was written using the AutoCAD® Raster Design software installed on the AutoCAD® software and all content refers to the AutoCAD software unless otherwise noted.

This introduction covers the following topics:

- Course Objectives
- Prerequisites
- Using This Courseware
- Exercise Files
- Installing the Downloaded Exercise Files
- Software Ribbon Display Issue
- Notes, Tips, and Warnings
- Feedback

This courseware is complementary to the software documentation. For detailed explanations of features and functionality, refer to the Help in the software.

Course Objectives

After completing this course, you will be able to:

- Insert and create images.
- Tile, save, and export images.
- Work with multispectral images.
- Correlate and rubbersheet images.
- Enhance the appearance of images.
- Edit images.
- Work with DEM data.
- Convert raster to vector.

Prerequisites

This course is designed for the student that is new to the AutoCAD Raster Design software.

It is recommended that you have a working knowledge of:

- Creating, opening, and saving drawing files; changing the display of a drawing by zooming and panning; displaying and docking toolbars; saving and restoring named views; using object snaps; and managing layers and controlling layer visibility.
- Microsoft® Windows®

Using This Courseware

The lessons are independent of each other. However, it is recommended that you complete these lessons in the order in which they are presented unless you are familiar with the concepts and functionality described in the lessons.

Each chapter contains:

- **Lessons** - Usually two or more lessons in each chapter.
- **Exercises** - Practical, real-world examples for you to practice using the functionality you have just learned. Each exercise contains step-by-step procedures and graphics to help you complete the exercise successfully.

Downloading and Installing the Exercise Files

The Exercise Files page contains a link to all of the data that you need to complete the exercises. Type the link into a web browser to download the files.

To install the data files for the exercises:

1. Type the link (provided on the Exercise Files page), into a web browser and download the .EXE file containing the Exercise Files.

2. Extract the .EXE file to C:\. This should be a directory for which you have read\write privileges for your user account. A folder called *C:\AutoCAD Raster Design 2017 Essentials Exercise Files* is created, containing the files that are required for each exercise.

Software Ribbon Display Issue

After the AutoCAD Raster Design software has been installed, if the Raster Tools tab does not display in the Ribbon when the software is launched, do the following:

1. In the Command Line, enter **CUILOAD**. Press ENTER.

2. In the Load/Unload Customizations dialog box, browse to *C:\Program Files\Autodesk\AutoCAD Raster Design 2017\UserDataCache\Support*.

3. Select AecCo.cuix. Click Open.

4. In the Load/Unload Customizations dialog box, click Load.

5. Select AUTOCADRASTERDESIGN. Click Close. The Raster Tools tab is added to the Ribbon.

Notes, Tips, and Warnings

Throughout this courseware, notes, tips, and warnings are called out for special attention.

Notes contain guidelines, constraints, and other explanatory information.

Tips provide information to enhance your productivity.

Warnings provide information about actions that might result in the loss of data, system failures, or other serious consequences.

Feedback

We always welcome feedback on Autodesk Official Training Courseware. After completing this course, if you have suggestions for improvements or want to report an error in the book or with the Exercise Files, please send your comments to *feedback@ascented.com*.

Exercise Files

To download the exercise files for this student guide, use the following steps:

1. Type the URL shown in the following image into the address bar of your Internet browser. The URL must be typed **exactly as shown**. If you are using an ASCENT ebook, you can click on the link to download the file.

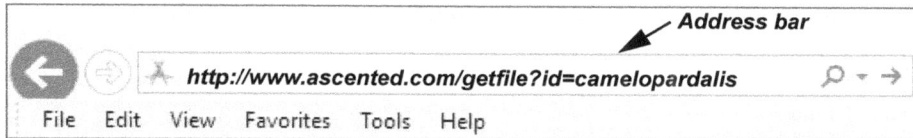

Address bar

http://www.ascented.com/getfile?id=camelopardalis

File   Edit   View   Favorites   Tools   Help

2. Press <Enter> to download the .ZIP file that contains the Exercise Files.

3. Once the download is complete, unzip the file to a local folder. The unzipped file contains an .EXE file.

4. Double-click on the .EXE file and follow the instructions to automatically install the Exercise Files on the C:\ drive of your computer.

   Do not change the location in which the Exercise Files folder is installed. Doing so can cause errors when completing the exercises in this student guide.

http://www.ascented.com/getfile?id=camelopardalis

Inserting and Creating Images

In this chapter you learn to work with raster images, including inserting and managing existing images and creating new ones.

By scanning paper drawings and storing them in raster format, you can more easily store, retrieve, and reproduce your drawings. You can use these scanned drawings in an AutoCAD® drawing file.

Objectives

After completing this chapter, you will be able to:

- Create a new image.
- Insert images in a drawing.
- Manage images in a drawing.
- Mask and crop an image.

Lesson: Creating a New Image

Overview

You use AutoCAD® Raster Design tools to work with raster images as you would use AutoCAD® tools to work with vectors. In this lesson you learn the basic concepts of working with raster images and how to create a new image.

```
┌─ Default Image Properties ─────────────────────────────────┐
│ Width:                                                     │
│    [3000        ]  Pixels    [10.0000    ]   Inches        │
│ Height:                                                    │
│    [3000        ]  Pixels    [10.0000    ]   Inches        │
│ Density:                                                   │
│    [300.0000    ]   pixels per    [Inches          ▼]      │
│                                                            │
│ ┌─ Default Color Type ─────────────────────────────────┐  │
│ │   ⦿ Bitonal (1-bit)        ○ Indexed color (8-bit)   │  │
│ │   ○ Grayscale (8-bit)      ○ True color (32-bit)     │  │
│ └──────────────────────────────────────────────────────┘  │
│ ┌─ Dialog Options ─────────────────────────────────────┐  │
│ │          ☑ Show new image dialog                     │  │
│ └──────────────────────────────────────────────────────┘  │
└────────────────────────────────────────────────────────────┘
```

In the process of learning how to create a new image, you learn the terminology used to describe raster images, as well as the properties of an image and how they are set.

Objectives

After completing this lesson, you will be able to:

- Describe the differences between raster and vector information.
- List and describe the properties of a raster image.
- Describe the default image settings and other guidelines for using raster images.
- Create a new image.

About Raster Images

Raster

A raster file is a series of dots, also called pixels, that form an image, as shown in the following illustration. This type of data is produced when you scan a paper drawing, blueprint, or photograph.

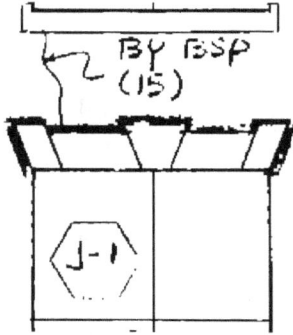

Raster data is not stored in a DWG™ file, but in a separate raster file that is attached to the drawing. This is similar to working with XREFs.

Vector

A vector is a mathematical object with precise direction and length, but without a specific location. Vector data is stored as XYZ coordinates that form points, lines, areas, and volumes as shown in the following illustration. It is used to store discrete, well-defined data that can be delimited.

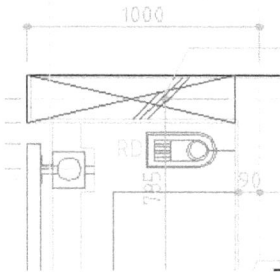

Raster Image Frame

The frame for a raster image is the rectangular vector object that surrounds the image. You can select the raster image frame by clicking it or using an AutoCAD selection method. The raster image frame is the only information that is saved in the DWG file.

Example

You need to draw new details that are unique to a project and reuse details from a previous project. To do so, scan the older details as raster data that can be edited using AutoCAD Raster Design commands, and draw the new details as vector data using AutoCAD commands. The resulting combination is called a hybrid drawing.

About Image Properties

A raster image that has been created or inserted in a drawing has several properties that are important when editing the image or working with multiple images. In the Raster Tools tab, in the Manage & View panel, click Manage... to open the Image Manager and view the image properties, as shown in the following illustration.

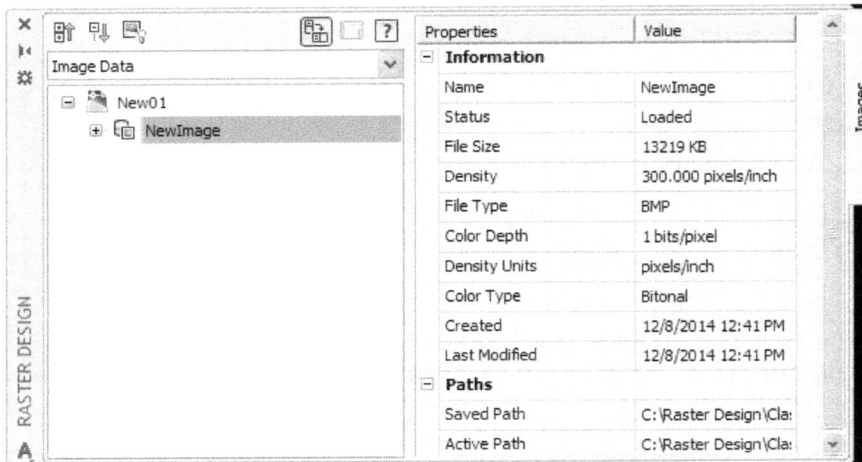

Pixels

A pixel is a single square dot on the screen. Pixels combine to form raster images and can be assigned different colors or shades of gray individually. The image pixel size varies depending on the resolution of the image. For example, a 2x2 pixel in a 400 dpi image is one quarter of the area of a 2x2 pixel in a 200 dpi image.

Resolution

The resolution of an image is the number of dots per unit at which an image has been scanned or created. The more dots used per unit, the higher the resolution.

Color Depth

The color depth of an image is the amount of information that is stored with each pixel to define its color or shade. The following table describes the color depths that are used in the AutoCAD Raster Design software.

Color Depth	Image Type	Available Colors
1 bit	Bitonal (black and white)	Two colors (one of which is a background or transparent color).
4 bit	Color	16 colors.
8 bit	Grayscale	256 shades of gray.
8 bit	Color	256 colors.
16 bit	Grayscale	65,536 shades of gray.

Color Depth	Image Type	Available Colors
24 bit	Color	16,777,216 colors.
32 bit	Color	16,777,216 colors. This is the same number of colors as 24 bit, but they are aligned in the palette differently to permit more efficient access to the color data.

Example

You need to scan a document that you want to use in a new project. For best results, you can scan the design documents (such as floor plans, schematic diagrams, and other linework), as bitonal images at 300 dpi (dots per inch). Many AutoCAD Raster Design commands are optimized for 300 dpi.

Creating Images

When you create a raster image, you can select the properties for the new image. This section suggests guidelines that can be followed when creating images.

Defaults

You can set the defaults in the AutoCAD Raster Design Options dialog box if you are going to create multiple images using the same values. If required, you can override any of the defaults as you create a new image, as shown in the following illustration. In the Raster Tools tab, in the Insert & Write panel, REM panel, or Vectorize & Recognize Text panel, click the Options arrow in the lower right corner to open the AutoCAD Raster Design Options dialog box.

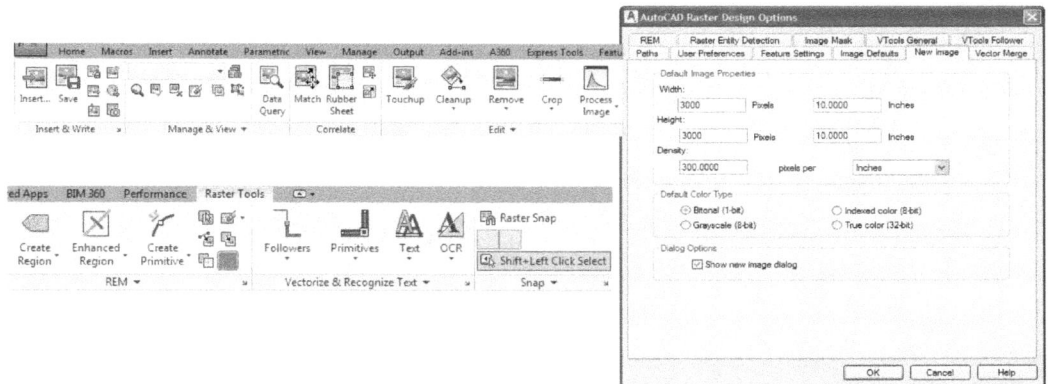

Guidelines for Using Raster Images

A raster image has specific constraints when used in an AutoCAD drawing file. Most of the constraints involve editing capabilities.

Editing Methods

When selecting an editing method, note the following:

- Raster data can only be edited using commands from the AutoCAD Raster Design software.
- Vector data can only be edited using AutoCAD commands, such as Move or Copy.
- The frame of a raster image is vector information and should be edited using AutoCAD commands.

Example

You want to work with raster images that combine the elements of existing scans and merge vector data to create a set of as-built drawings. To ensure consistency between images, you can use the settings in the New Image tab in the AutoCAD Raster Design Options dialog box to create defaults for any new images. You can then create a new image and merge its raster and vector data.

If you did not set the defaults before starting, you need to verify the image properties each time a new image is created, wasting time and increasing the possibility of errors.

Exercise: Create a New Image

In this exercise, you will create a new raster image by defining and saving the new image.

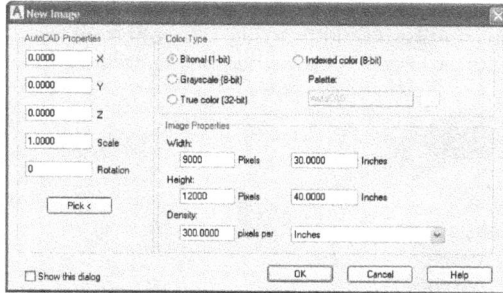

The completed image

1. Open ...\Creating a New Image\New01.dwg.

2. In the Raster Tools tab, in the Insert & Write panel, click New.

3. In the New Image dialog box, specify the settings for the new image:

   - Under AutoCAD Properties, verify that the X, Y, and Z values are set to 0.
   - Verify that the Scale value is 1.

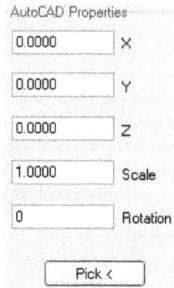

   - Under Image Properties, verify that Density is set to 300 and pixels per is set to Inches.

4. Set the Width to 30 inches and the Height to 40 inches. To complete the Height entry you must click in any other area.

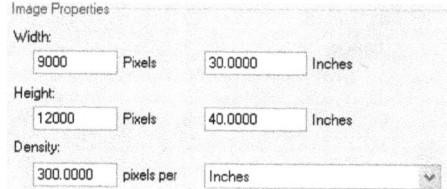

   - Click OK.

5. In the Raster Tools tab, in the Insert & Write panel, click Save As.

6. In the Save As dialog box, for File name, accept the name **NewImage**. For Files of type, select Windows Bitmap (*.bmp, *.dib, *.rle) from the list.

7. Click Save.

Lesson: Inserting Images

Overview

In this lesson you learn how to place raster images in an AutoCAD drawing file. Different tools for image insertion are introduced, as well as the concepts required to ensure that the images are placed accurately using coordinate transformations.

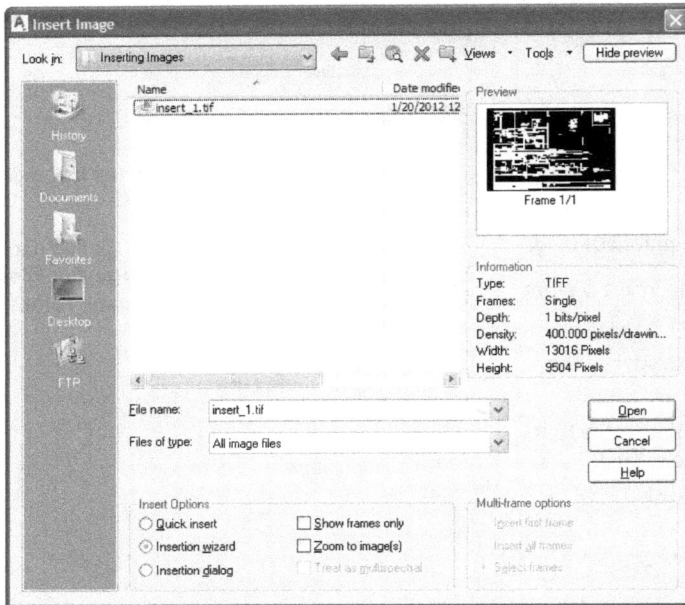

Although the AutoCAD® software can work with scanned or other digital images, it does not include tools for accurately locating and sizing these images. You can use the AutoCAD Raster Design Insert command to insert an image at a specific insertion point, scale, and rotation in your drawing. You can also use it to perform coordinate transformations to match images and drawings with differing coordinate systems.

Objectives

After completing this lesson, you will be able to:

- Determine when to use a raster image and identify the types of raster images that can be used.
- Describe an inserted raster.
- Define correlation and identify correlation data sources.
- Define coordinate transformation and its associated terms.
- Decide how to correctly scan a document.
- Decide how to correctly insert a raster image.
- Insert an image using the Insertion Wizard.

Working with Raster Images

In every discipline, information is often stored on paper. In addition, many newer types of information are provided in digital formats. Information that can be used as raster images includes:

- Paper-based, as-built drawings
- Archive photographs
- Historical documentation
- Hand-sketched concept drawings
- Digital camera photographs
- Satellite data
- Digital elevation models (DEMs)
- Renderings of a design

When you use these types of information as raster files, you do not need to recreate or redraw the data.

Example

You are renovating an existing office building and you scan the as-built drawings to use them as a background for designing the new working spaces. By using a raster image for the as-built drawings, you do not need to redraw the existing plan set. A scanned floor plan is shown in the following illustration.

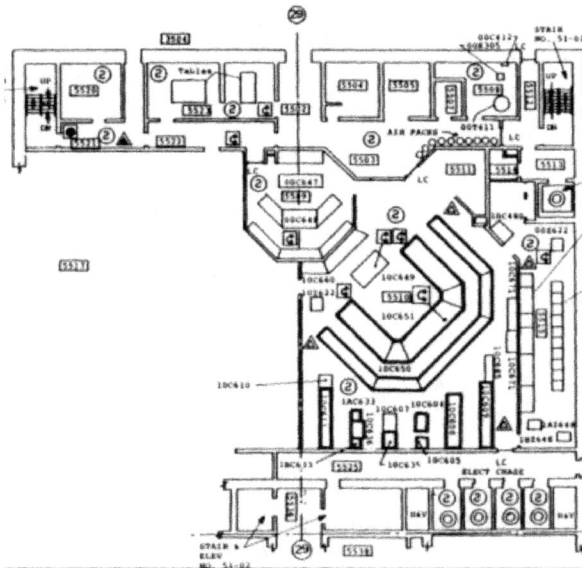

About Inserting Raster Images

You can use one of the following methods to insert an image:

Method	Description
Quick insert	Inserts an image using the default values in the image header or set in the AutoCAD Raster Design Options dialog box.
Insertion wizard	Uses a wizard to step through the insertion process and provides guidance in selecting the options available for inserting images.
Insertion dialog	Presents the same information as the Insertion wizard in a tabbed dialog box.

Select a method under Insert Options in the Insert Image dialog box as shown in the following illustration.

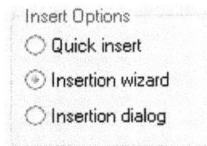

Insertion Point

The insertion point incorporates the X, Y, and Z coordinates where the image is located, and is located in the lower-left corner of the image as shown in the following illustration.

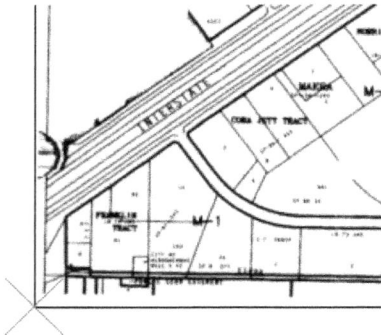

Scale

The scale factor is used to resize an image based on its original size. For example, a scale of 2 makes the image twice as large in the drawing as it is in the original image file. Typically, a scale is applied to an image to match existing geometry or other images.

Rotation

Rotation is the angle at which an image is revolved about its insertion point as shown in the following illustration.

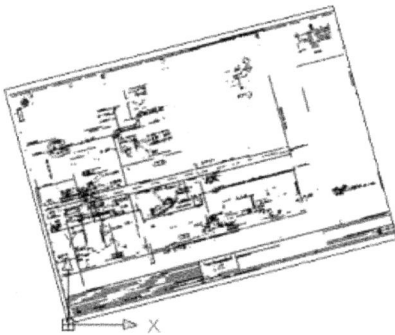

Quick Insert

When you have many images to insert and want to use the same settings for each one, you can use the Quick Insert method. Note the following when using Quick Insert:

- It does not enable you to change the correlation data.
- The defaults for Quick Insert can be set in the AutoCAD Raster Design Options dialog box.

Image Insertion Dialog Box

You can use several options in the Image Insertion dialog box when inserting an image, as shown in the following illustration.

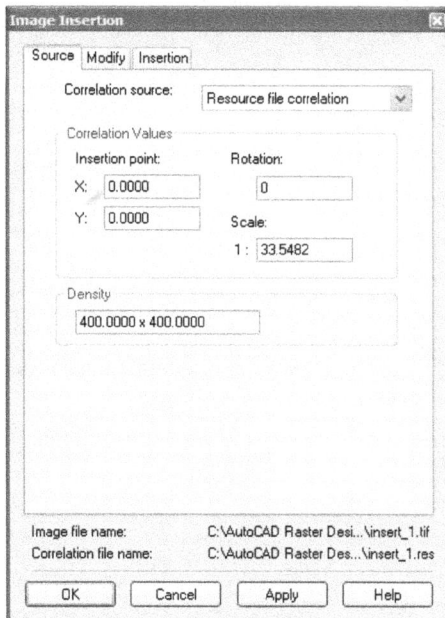

Key Points

Note the following when you use the Image Insertion dialog box:

- Multiple tabs are available and you should review all of the settings on each tab.
- The defaults for the dialog box can be set in the AutoCAD Raster Design Options dialog box.
- If you have selected a DEM file, or you are collating several images as a multispectral image, the Assign Color Map tab is available. If you are using any other image type, this tab is not available.
- If your current drawing has an assigned coordinate system and you are using the AutoCAD® Map 3D software, the AutoCAD® Land Desktop software, or the AutoCAD® Civil 3D® software, the Transform tab is available. If the current drawing does not have an assigned coordinate system, or you are using another Autodesk product, this tab is not available.

Example

When you scan an 8" x 10" photograph, the resulting image has its insertion point, scale, and rotation set to the defaults from the scanner. Typically, the lower-left corner of the image is the insertion point, the scale is 1, and the rotation angle is 0. The image displays as it was scanned in terms of its size and orientation.

About Correlation Data

You must consider several factors when inserting an image, especially its correlation. If the insertion point, scale, and rotation of the image do not match the existing drawing, you must correlate the image after its insertion. The following terms are used when correlating an image during insertion.

Correlation Data

Correlation data includes the insertion point, rotation, and scale (as shown in the following illustration), which are used to match an image to a drawing.

Correlation Values

Insertion point:		Rotation:
X:	0.0000	0
Y:	0.0000	Scale:
		1 : 33.5482

Correlation File

This file is the source of the correlation data for an image and is saved as a separate file. The two types of supported correlation files are: resource and world files.

Correlation source: Resource file correlation

Correlation Options

When you insert an image, the AutoCAD Raster Design software searches all of the available correlation files for the image and displays them under Correlation Source. Depending on the type of image being inserted, and whether a resource or world file exists for the image, the following sources might be listed:

Option	Description
Image File	Specific types of images in which the correlation data can be saved as part of the image file. These file formats include RLC, IG4, IGS, GeoTags in GeoTIFF, and HDR File in SPOT.
Resource File	A file created by the AutoCAD Raster Design Export command. Resource files have a RES file extension.
World File	A file created by the AutoCAD Raster Design Export command for all image formats. World files have different file extensions, depending on their file formats.

Example

You scan an aerial photograph to be used as the background for several drawings. By saving a correlation file with this image, you do not need to manually correlate the scan for each drawing.

About Coordinate Transformation

Image data for AEC and GIS projects can be gathered from many different sources. However, not all of these sources are going to match the coordinate systems used in your drawings. This section defines the terms encountered when matching projection systems between images and drawings.

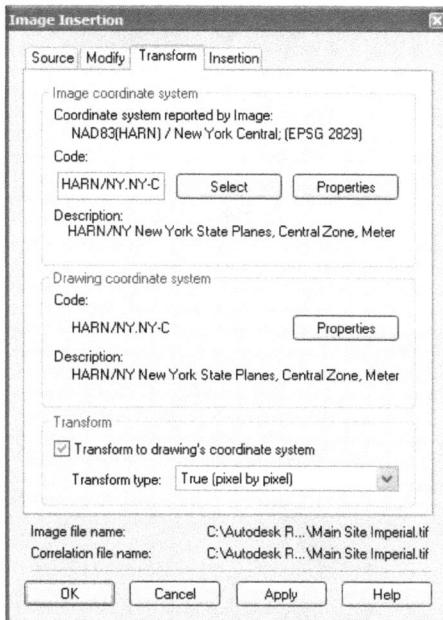

Coordinate Systems

A coordinate system is a description of the origin of your drawing, the drawing's projection system, and the units used in the drawing. Most maps use a type of coordinate system to represent the curvature of the Earth's surface on a flat plane, such as a sheet of paper.

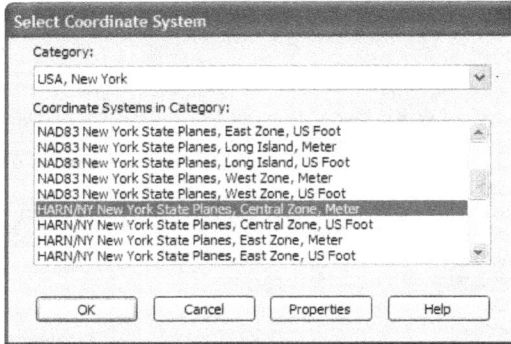

Coordinate systems can only be assigned to drawings in the AutoCAD Map 3D software, AutoCAD Land Desktop software, or AutoCAD Civil 3D software.

Coordinate Transformation

The assigned coordinate systems enable you to combine and work with data from images and drawings that use different coordinate systems. When you insert the image into your drawing, it is automatically converted to the global coordinate system of the current drawing. This operation is called coordinate transformation.

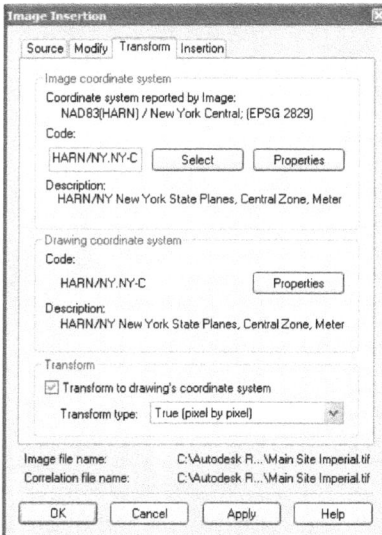

Example

You have a drawing that is set up with a state plane projection using US feet as the units. You acquire a satellite image of the area that has been set up with a UTM projection and the base units are meters. You can use a coordinate transformation when inserting this image to ensure that the areas match.

Acquiring Raster Images

Although there are many sources for digital data, scanning is the most common way to get paper plans into a raster format. By scanning paper drawings and storing them in raster format, you make it easier to store, retrieve, reproduce, and reuse the information.

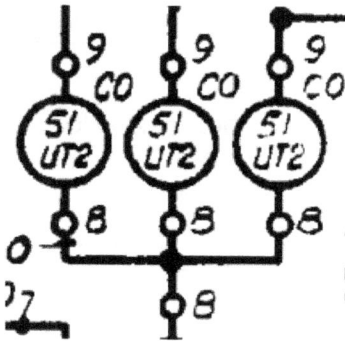

Guidelines for Scanning Documents

Most image types are supported by the AutoCAD Raster Design software. This includes most file formats as well as binary, grayscale, and true color images.

The following guidelines can be used when scanning existing documents:

- Check the resolution on the scanner to ensure that it is appropriate for the application of the raster image. For example, the text recognition tools in the AutoCAD Raster Design software are optimized for 300 dpi images.
- Check the color depth on the scanner to ensure that it is appropriate for the type of document being scanned. For example, if the document is a floor plan, it should be scanned as a bitonal (black-and-white line art) raster image rather than as a color image.
- After you scan your drawings, you should organize the raster files in a drawing management system that is easy to use, reliable, and ensures the integrity of your data.

Inserting Raster Images

Insertion Options

You can only use one command to insert an image in the AutoCAD Raster Design software. However, you can control the behavior and defaults for this command using the AutoCAD Raster Design Options dialog box.

Option	Description
Show frames only	Inserts the image and toggles the main portion of the image off so that only the frames are visible. This is useful when loading many large images at the same time, because the graphics processor is not overloaded with information.
Zoom to image(s)	When the image is inserted, the drawing zooms to display the entire new image.
Treat as multispectral	Aggregates several images into a single multispectral image.

Use the check boxes at the bottom of the Insert Image dialog box to select these options.

Guidelines for Inserting Images

Note the following when inserting images:

- Images are always placed on the current layer. Therefore, you need to review the layer settings before inserting an image.
- Show frames only and Zoom to image(s) can be used with any image type.
- If any information, such as correlation data, is missing when you insert an image, the defaults set in the AutoCAD Raster Design Options dialog box are used.
- You must use the AutoCAD Map 3D software, the AutoCAD Land Desktop software, or the AutoCAD Civil 3D software to perform a coordinate transformation.

Exercise: Use the Insertion Wizard to Insert an Image

In this exercise, you will insert an image using all four pages of the Insertion Wizard.

The completed exercise

1. Open ...\Inserting Images\insert_1.dwg.

2. In the Application Menu, select Drawing Utilities and then select Units.

   NOTE: Depending on which AutoCAD-based product you are using, the Units command might be found in a different menu.

3. In the Drawing Units dialog box, set the following units:

   - Under Length, for Type, select Decimal.
   - Under Insertion scale, for Units to scale inserted content, select Meters.
   - Click OK.

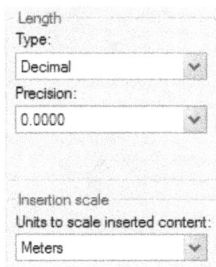

4. In the Raster Tools tab, in the Insert & Write panel, click Insert.

5. In the Insert Image dialog box, specify the insert parameters:

   - Under Insert Options, click Insertion wizard, if required.
   - Browse to ...\Inserting Images folder in your exercise files folder.
   - Click insert_1.tif.
   - Under Insert Options, click Zoom to image(s).

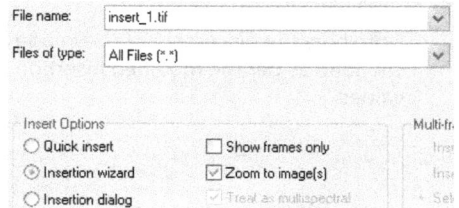

6. Click Open.

7. In the Pick Correlation Source dialog box, verify that the Correlation source is set to Resource file correlation.

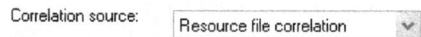

8. Click Next.

9. In the Modify Correlation Values dialog box, under Units, for Image units, select Meters.

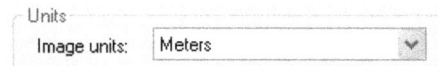

10. Click Apply and click Next.

11. Move the Insertion dialog box to the right side of the screen:

- For X, enter **25** and for Y, enter **25**. Click Apply.
- For Rotation, enter **15**. Click Apply.
- For Scale, enter **20**. Click Apply.

Correlation Values

Insertion point:		Rotation:
X:	25.0000	15
Y:	25.0000	Scale:
Z:	0.0000	1 : 20.0000

12. Click Finish.

Note how the placement of the image has changed as per the modified insertion values.

Lesson: Managing Images in a Drawing

Overview

In this lesson you learn how to use the Images Manager to manage images in a drawing. The Images tab in the Image Manager has tools that can be used to display and edit raster image properties, edit the saved file paths, and change the display order of the images.

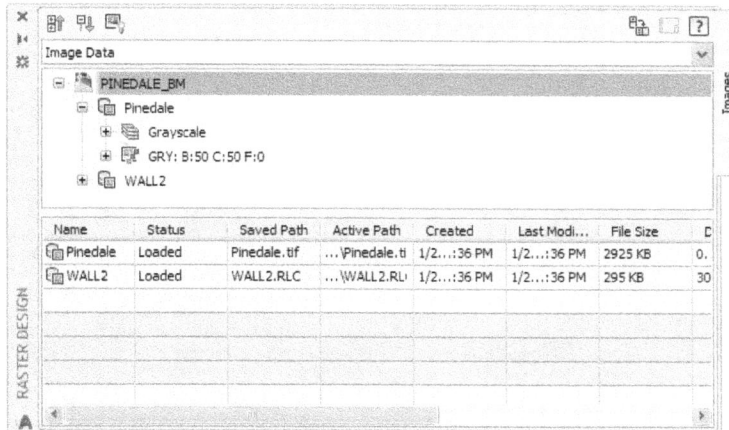

A drawing can contain multiple raster images. Using traditional AutoCAD tools, you can only display the properties of one image at a time. However, using the Images tab in the Image Manager, you can review information about all of the images in the current drawing and perform other management tasks.

Objectives

After completing this lesson, you will be able to:

- Describe image management.
- View information about, and organize the images in, the current drawing.
- Review information about images in the current drawing using the Image Manager.
- Change the display order of images in a drawing using the Image Manager.

About Image Management

Image Manager

The Image Manager displays information about the current drawing. With the Images tab, you can manage multiple image insertions, color maps, and related data. Two views are available in a drop-down list: Image Data and Image Insertions.

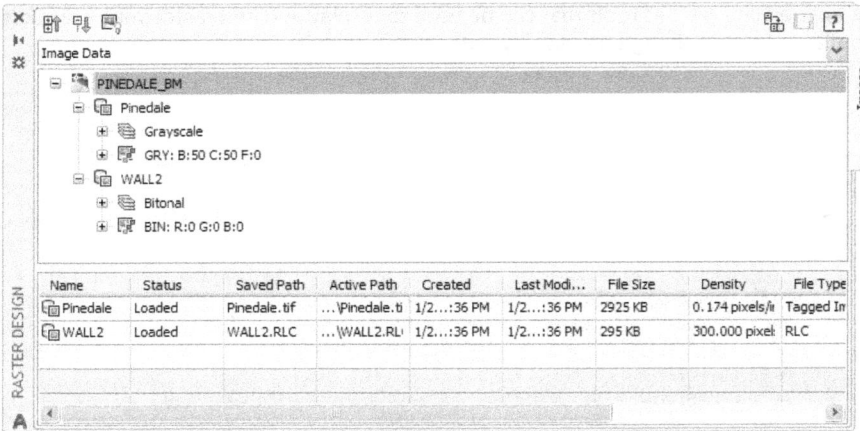

Image Data View

Use the Image Data view to work with the image files (also called image data definitions) that are attached to the current drawing. This is useful when creating new insertions of previously attached files and detaching, reloading, or changing the saved path of a previously inserted image.

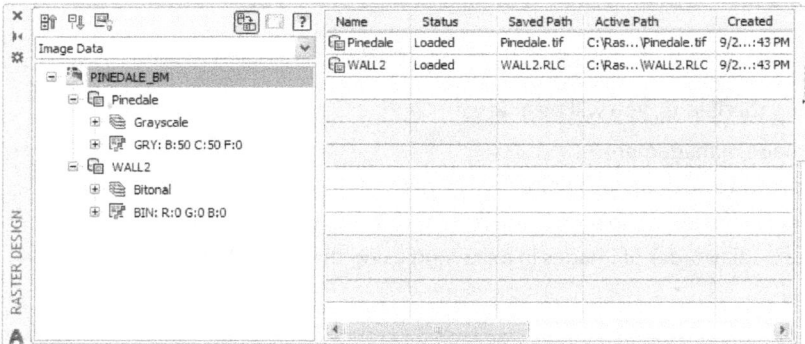

Image Insertions View

Use the Image Insertions view to manage inserted images and their color maps, including changing the properties of an image and editing a color map. If you insert the same image file more than once, each image name includes a distinguishing number, such as View:1 or View:2.

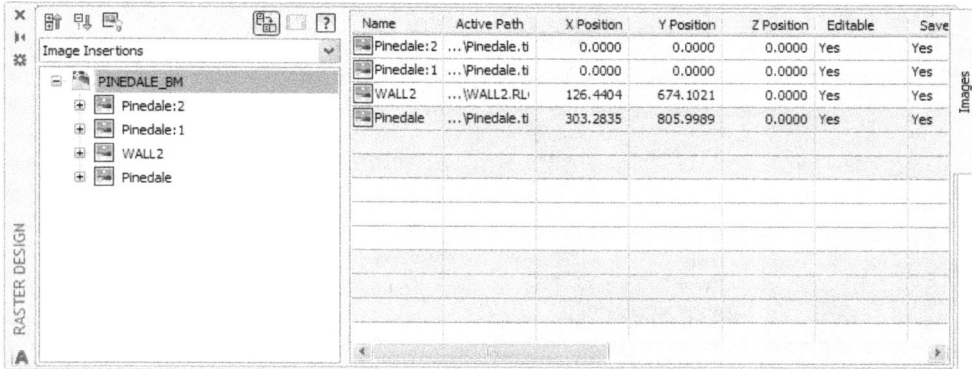

Name	Active Path	X Position	Y Position	Z Position	Editable	Save
Pinedale:2	...\Pinedale.ti	0.0000	0.0000	0.0000	Yes	Yes
Pinedale:1	...\Pinedale.ti	0.0000	0.0000	0.0000	Yes	Yes
WALL2	...\WALL2.RL	126.4404	674.1021	0.0000	Yes	Yes
Pinedale	...\Pinedale.ti	303.2835	805.9989	0.0000	Yes	Yes

Example

You have a drawing to which several images have been associated and you want to verify which images are used in the drawing. You can use the Image Data view to display the image files that are attached to the drawing and the Image Insertions view to display the files that have been inserted in the drawing.

Image Management Tools

You can use several tools in the Images tab in the Image Manager to edit and manage your raster images, including changing color maps, detaching images, changing file paths, and editing the display order.

The following terms are used when working with the image management tools.

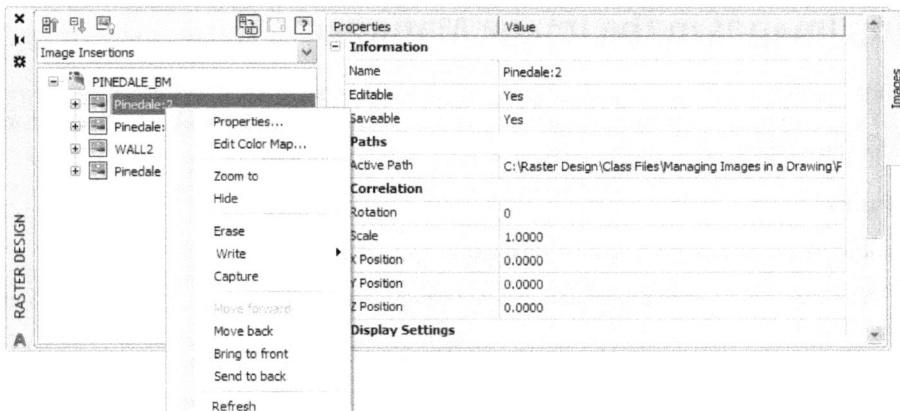

Properties	Value
Information	
Name	Pinedale:2
Editable	Yes
Saveable	Yes
Paths	
Active Path	C:\Raster Design\Class Files\Managing Images in a Drawing\F
Correlation	
Rotation	0
Scale	1.0000
X Position	0.0000
Y Position	0.0000
Z Position	0.0000
Display Settings	

Display Order

The front-to-back display of images in the drawing is controlled by the order in which images are listed in Image Insertions view in the Image Manager. This is also called the display order. The first image listed is on top of all of the other images that it overlaps, and the one listed last is behind them.

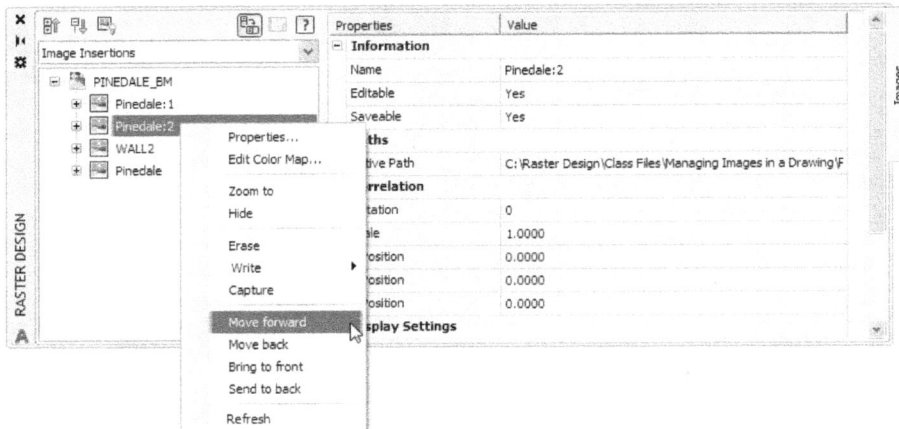

Active Path

The active path is the location from which the current image file is being loaded. This is different from the saved path. Note that if the requested image cannot be found in the saved location, the image file might have been moved, copied, or deleted from the saved location.

Example

You have a drawing with an attached image that was sent to you via e-mail. However, because the folder structure on your computer is different from the one used to create the drawing, the image's saved path is not correct. You can use the Images tab in the Image Manager to change the saved path to be the image file's new location.

Managing Images in the Image Manager

Although a great deal of information displays in the image management system, reviewing image data is fairly simple in the Image Manager. You can also use the Image Manager to change the display order for the images.

Key Points

When using the Images tab in the Image Manager, note the following:

- In the Raster Tools tab, in the Manage & View panel, click Manage... to open the Image Manager in the Images tab.
- Use the View list to switch between the Image Data and Image Insertions views.
- Right-click on any image name for additional image management tools, such as changing the Saved Path for the image.

About Image Display Order

Raster images display in the order in which you insert them. You can manually change the display order if you want one image to be displayed on top of another. Additionally, you can set the raster image to be displayed beneath vectors.

Changing the Display Order

You can change the display order of images in the current drawing in the following ways:

- Select and right-click on the frame of the Image. Click Draw Order and select the required option.
- In the Home tab, in the expanded Modify panel, in the Draw Order flyout, select an option and select the image to change.
- Right-click on the image name in the Image Insertions view in the Images tab in the Image Manager. Select the required option.

Editing Images

When you edit an image, it might seem to be placed on top of other images and vectors. In fact, the image display order has not been changed. Use the AutoCAD REGEN command to display the images and vectors in their correct order.

Exercise: View Image Information in the Image Manager

In this exercise, you will learn how to view information about an existing raster image using the Images tab in the Image Manager.

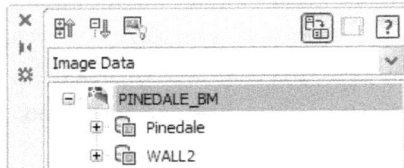

The completed exercise

1. Open ...\Managing Images in a Drawing\ PINEDALE_BM.dwg.

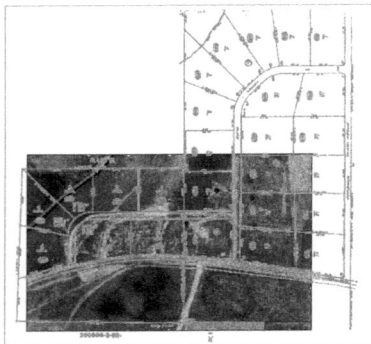

2. In the Raster Tools tab, in the Manage & View panel, click Manage to open the Image Manager.

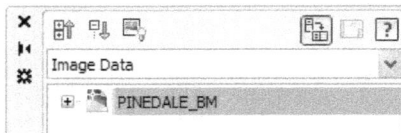

3. Click the plus sign (+) in the Image Manager next to PINEDALE_BM to display the images in the current drawing.

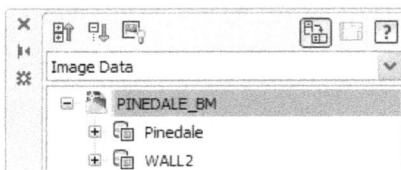

4. Click PINEDALE_BM in the list to display its properties in the Images tab.

5. Scroll across the columns to view the displayed properties.

Name	Status	Saved Path	Active Path	Created	Last
Pinedale	Loaded	Pinedale. tif	...\Pinedale.ti	1/2...:36 PM	1/2...
WALL2	Loaded	WALL2.RLC	...\WALL2.RL	1/2...:36 PM	1/2...

6. Right-click on any of the column titles to revise the layout of the Image Manager. Clear Active Path and Created. Verify that the Created column is removed.

Name	Status	Saved Path	Last Modi...	File Size	
Pinedale	Loaded	Pinedale.tif	1/2...:36 PM	2925 KB	0.
WALL2	Loaded	WALL2.RLC	1/2...:36 PM	295 KB	30

7. Close the Image Manager.

Exercise: Change Image Display Properties

If images overlap, you can use the Images tab in the Images Manager to change their display order. You can control which image is fully displayed and which is in the background. You can change the display properties, such as transparency settings.

The completed exercise

1. Open ...\Managing Images in a Drawing\ Aerial01.dwg.

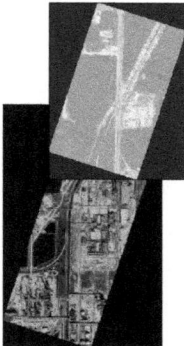

2. If the Image Manager does not display, in the Raster Tools tab, in the Manage & View panel, click Manage.

3. In the Image Manager, in the View list, select Image Insertions.

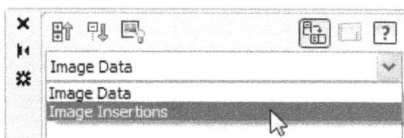

4. Expand Aerial01. Right-click on 1i07b and click Send to back.

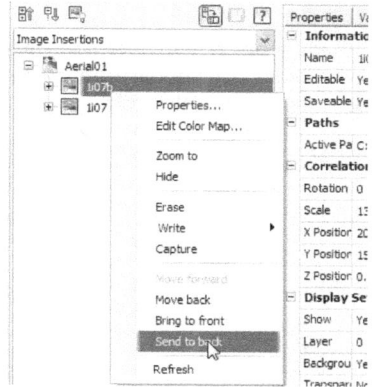

5. Right-click on 1i07. Click Properties.

6. In the Properties palette, change the transparency color:

    - Under Raster Settings, click in the Transparent color area.
    - Click the settings box.

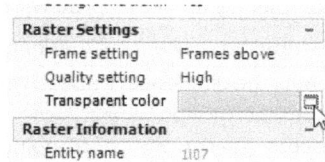

    - In the Transparent Color dialog box, click Select.
    - Click in the black portion of the image.

    - Click OK.

7. Close the Properties palette. Close the Image Manager.

Lesson: Masking and Cropping Images

Overview

For many projects, you might only need a portion of a raster image, such as one area in an aerial photograph or one detail from a scanned drawing. In this lesson you learn how to use the Mask and Crop tools to select the portions of an image that you want to display.

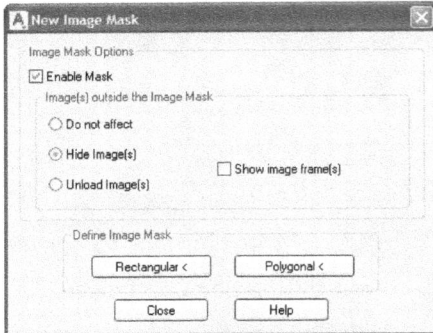

By reducing the size of images in a drawing, you can save time opening, viewing, and printing the drawing.

Objectives

After completing this lesson, you will be able to:

- Describe the concepts of masking images.
- Identify the differences between masking and clipping an image, as well as guidelines to use when applying an image mask.
- Describe the concepts of cropping images.
- Determine whether to use the Mask or Crop tools when preparing images in a drawing.

About Masking Images

You can use image masking and clipping to hide portions of the display of a raster image. Clipping is available in the AutoCAD software in the Raster Tools tab, in the expanded Manage & View panel. Masking is unique to the AutoCAD Raster Design software and can be used on multiple images simultaneously.

Image Mask

An image mask plots and displays a subset of the images in your drawing. The Mask command visually trims an image by hiding or unloading the portions of the image that are completely outside the mask boundary. You can mask images using a rectangular or polygonal boundary.

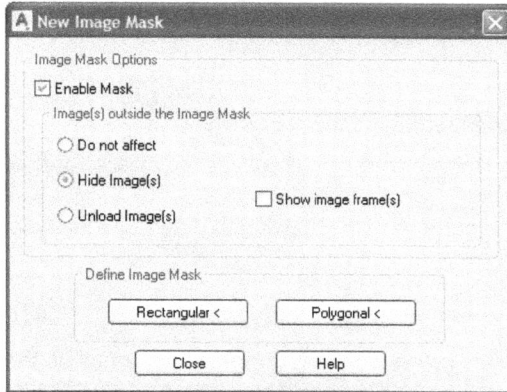

Image Clip

When you clip an image, the portions of the image that are outside the clip boundary are covered by the transparency color and hidden from view. A clip is a display-only feature, which is used for viewing and plotting.

Example

You tiled several aerial photographs for the design of a long corridor project. You only need the information that falls along the corridor. Therefore, you can create a polygonal mask over all of the images to hide the raster data that is not required for the project.

Guidelines for Creating an Image Mask

You sometimes need to hide portions of an image. This section discusses the guidelines can be used when determining which portion of an image to hide, and whether to use a mask or a clip.

Clipping and Masking Images

To use an image mask or clip, note the following:

- An image mask can be converted into an image clip, but not vice-versa.
- Image mask and clip boundaries are drawing objects that can be modified using grip editing or other editing commands.
- Image masks and clips are display-only features and do not change the image file. Both features hide, rather than remove, the raster data.

Masking an Image

To use an image mask, note the following when setting up the mask:

- View the images in the drawing and determine how the ones outside the masked area are affected.
- Determine the area to be masked and the purpose of the drawing to determine the type of boundary that should be applied.

Example

You are creating plan and profile sheets that are going to display an aerial photograph in the background of the plan view. You can use an image mask to hide the portions of the aerial photograph that extend beyond the project area. To provide visual consistency in the plan and profile sheet, you can use a rectangular mask boundary, and hide all of the images that fall outside the masked area.

Since the images in the aerial photographs might display in other plan and profile sheets, you do not want to modify the underlying raster images. Therefore, you need to use a mask rather than editing the images directly.

About Cropping Images

When you crop a raster image, you select a portion of the image. The pixel data outside the crop is deleted and the image frame size is adjusted automatically. A crop permanently modifies an image. The following types of cropping regions are available:

- Linear
- Circular
- Rectangular
- Polygonal
- Diagonal

Example

You have a very large aerial photograph, but only a portion of it applies to your project. You can crop out the required portion of the image, removing the rest of the data. This results in a much smaller file that is easier to work with.

Whether to Crop or Mask an Image

Masking and cropping images can create similar results visually, but their affects on the image and drawing file can be quite different. This section provides guidelines that can be used when determining which type of command to use.

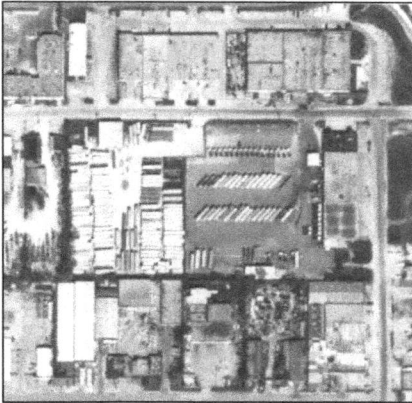

Image-Cropping Guidelines

- Unlike with masking or clipping, cropping permanently changes an image. You must use the Undo command during the same drawing session to remove an image crop.
- After you crop a raster image, you can save it to a new image file using the Save As command in the Raster Tools tab, in the Insert & Write panel.
- The images must always be rectangular. If you use an irregular cropping boundary, such as a circle or polygon, the area between the frame and the cropped region is filled with the background color. You can toggle on transparency to avoid wasting ink when printing.

An image that is created by cropping a larger image can itself be masked or clipped. This can be used to reduce backgrounds in an image that has been created using an irregular crop area, such as a circle.

Example

You want to reuse part of a scanned detail sheet for a different project. You only need one detail. Therefore, you remove the scanned border and title sheet by using the Crop command to delete the region around that detail. You then save the resulting image with a new filename.

You do not use a mask or clip, because doing so would not reduce the actual size of the file. The border would be retained in the image file.

Exercise: Mask Images

The Mask command plots and displays a subset of the images in your drawing. In this exercise, you create an image mask.

The completed exercise

1. Open ...\Masking and Cropping Images\ Aerial.dwg.

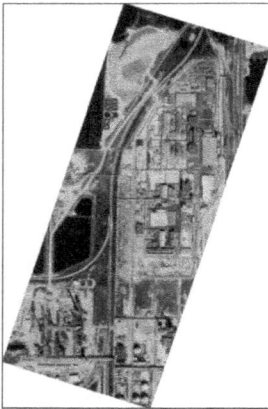

2. In the Raster Tools tab, expand the Manage & View tab, click Create Mask.

3. In the New Image Mask dialog box, under Define Image Mask, click Rectangular.

4. Define the rectangle:

   ▪ Enter **1080,3440** as the first corner point and press ENTER.
   ▪ Press ENTER to accept the default of 0 for the angle.
   ▪ Enter **735,4040** as the next corner point and press ENTER.

Exercise: Crop Raster Data Outside a Polygon

In this exercise, you will remove all of the raster information outside a selected polygonal region.

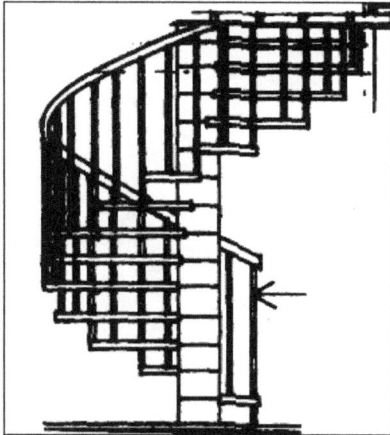

The completed exercise

1. Open ...\Masking and Cropping Images\ Cabin_09.dwg.

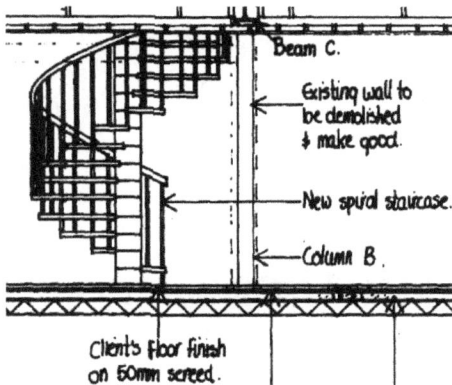

2. In the Raster Tools tab, in the Edit panel, expand Crop, and click Polygonal Region.

3. To define the polygon around the spiral staircase, click (minimum of three points) around the raster data that you want to preserve.

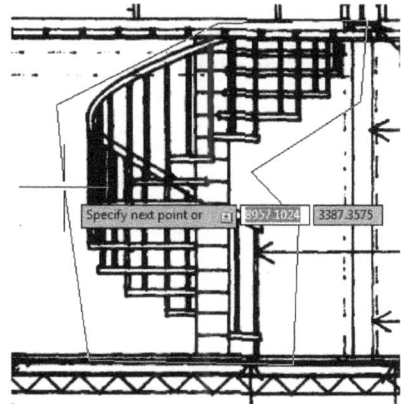

4. Press ENTER to close the polygon and crop the raster data.

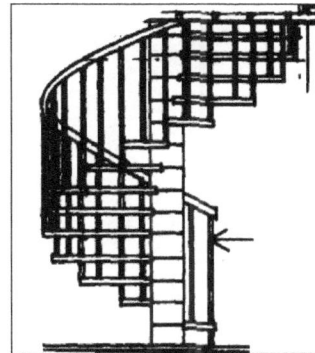

Chapter Summary

Having completed this chapter, you can:

- Create a new image.
- Insert images in a drawing.
- Manage images in a drawing.
- Mask and crop an image.

Tiling, Saving, and Exporting Images

In this chapter you learn how to create and insert images and how to save an image or export it to another file format. You can work with many raster images at the same time and create a correlation file using the Export tool.

Objectives

After completing this chapter, you will be able to:

- Work with tiled images.
- Save images.
- Export image files.

Lesson: Working with Multiple Images

Overview

In this lesson you learn how to set up multiple images to display a large area, and work on them as tiled images. If you want to convert multiple images into a single file, you can use the Merge tool. This converts the file format, color depth, and resolution to produce a single cohesive raster image.

Several editing and cleanup tools in the AutoCAD® Raster Design software only work on one image file at a time. By merging tiled images, you can work on all of the raster data for an area as one image file.

Objectives

After completing this lesson, you will be able to:

- Define the terms used when working with tiled images.
- Identify the terms used when merging images.
- Describe the methods used to select multiple images and determine when to merge images.
- Identify situations in which merging images is recommended.
- Merge several images and save the results as a new image file.

Working with Images and Frames

You can use tiled images when you need to work with more than one image to display information over a large area. The following terms are used when you are working with images and frames.

Tiled Images

Multiple images that are used to cover a large area are called tiled images. Note that this is not the same as tiling in a single image, such as the encoding used for TIFF images.

When working with tiled images, there are several options for displaying them and their frames.

Show/Hide Images

When you toggle the raster data in an image frame on/off, this is called showing or hiding an image. Hiding an image is similar to toggling off a layer in that the raster data cannot be seen. This is useful when you are dealing with a large amount of raster data, because the data for an image that is hidden does not need to be updated when you are zooming, panning, or manipulating the image frames.

Show Frames Only

You can set the Show Frames Only option when you insert images, which makes it faster to insert tiled images and to manage large amounts of data. Show Frames Only is useful for identifying the locations and sizes of tiled images, and you can use it with any of the insert methods.

Show/Hide Image Frames

In addition to being able to show or hide raster data, you can toggle the display of the image frames on/off. Toggling off the image frames before printing creates a cleaner-looking image.

Changing the Display of Image Frames

You can control the display of image frames using one of the following methods:

- In the Raster Tools tab, in the Manage & View panel, click Toggle Frames.
- In empty space in the drawing, right-click and click Image>Show Image Frame(s).

When you select one of these methods, the frames for all of the images toggle on/off in the drawing. You cannot toggle the frame for a single image on/off.

Example

You are setting up a drawing with several aerial photographs of a large site. If you insert the images with the Show Frames Only option toggled on, you can work with the image frames without having to display all of the raster data. For printing the drawing, you can show the images and hide the image frames.

About Merging Images

When merging images, you work with one or more source images and one destination image. The following definitions and tips are used when working with the images.

Source Image

The raster images that you merge are source images. They can be any file format and because the destination image controls the final color depth, resolution, and file format, their properties can be changed.

Destination Image

The destination image contains all of the source images when the merge is complete. There can only be one destination image for each merge. A merge uses the properties of the destination image.

Example

The as-built documents that you scanned for a large renovation project cover several pages. You can crop the borders from the scanned images, tile them, and merge them into a single raster image to use as the background for the renovation design.

Working with Multiple Images

When you are working with multiple images it can be difficult to select the images to edit. The following guidelines can be used to select images individually or as a group, and to determine whether images should be merged for ease of editing.

Selecting Images

You can select an image in the AutoCAD Raster Design software using the following methods:

- Click the image frame.
- Use AutoCAD® selection methods, such as Window or Crossing, to select several images at the same time.
- Press SHIFT and click inside the image frame.

If you use SHIFT + click to select an image and if there is only one image under the cursor, it is selected and a message displays in the Command Line. However, if there is more than one image under the cursor, the Image Select dialog box opens as shown in the following illustration.

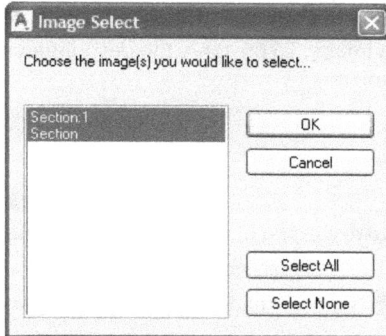

When the images you are working with cover a large portion of the drawing, it can be time-consuming to zoom and pan until you can easily select an image frame. Using the SHIFT + click method can greatly reduce the amount of editing time required when working with large images. A window or crossing selection method might not work on large images because the image frame might not be displayed at the current zoom level.

Guidelines for When to Merge Images

Sometimes you can have multiple images in one drawing file. The following guidelines can be used to determine when these images should be merged to form a single image:

- The images are tiled along their edges and represent different areas of the same project. For example, they could be different portions of a floor plan scanned from separate pages in a construction document set.
- The images are typically inserted in the same relative positions to each other, such as contiguous aerial photographs.
- Images that are going to be processed further for presentation purposes.

If your images are stacked at the same insertion point, such as a contour overlay on top of an aerial photograph, it is recommended that you keep them as separate images rather than merging them.

The Process of Merging Images

The following steps and guidelines can be used when preparing multiple images for merging. Following these steps before merging images helps to ensure predictable results from the merge.

Procedure: Merging Images

Use the following steps to prepare and merge multiple images:

1. Examine the images to be merged to determine which one is going to be the destination image. Note that the properties of the destination image dictate the properties of the image resulting from the merge.

2. If the destination image does not have the required properties, you can modify the destination image using other AutoCAD Raster Design editing tools, select a different image to be the destination image, or create a new image.

3. Once you have started the tool you are going to use to merge the images, select all of the source images before selecting the destination image. You can use any selection method, including Window or Crossing, or the SHIFT + click method.

4. When you complete the merge, save the resulting image. To preserve the destination image file as it was originally inserted, use the Save As tool.

Guidelines

When merging images, note the following:

- Any clip boundaries applied to the source images are respected in the final merged image.
- Any spaces resulting from the merge are filled with the transparency color.
- If the source images cover an area larger than the destination image, that image is expanded to cover the new area.

Exercise: Merge Images

In this exercise, you will merge several images into one destination image and save it with a new filename.

The completed exercise

1. Open ...\Merging Images\28sw.dwg.

   Six square images are placed adjacent to each other.

2. In the Raster Tools tab, in the expanded Edit panel, click Merge Images.

3. Select all of the six images available in the drawing. (Use the Window option to select all the images.)

4. Press ENTER.

5. Click the edge of the upper-left image as the destination image.

6. Press ENTER to erase the source images.

7. Click Yes at each of the prompts to detach the source images.

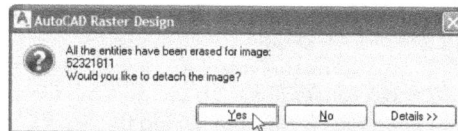

   The images are combined into a single image file. Note that all the individual edges are removed

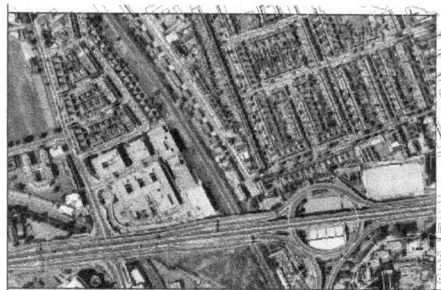

8. In the Raster Tools tab, in the Insert & Write panel, click Save As.

9. In the Save As dialog box, for File name, enter **523-ALL**.

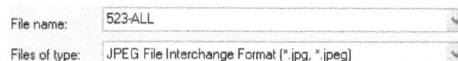

10. Click Save.

11. In the Encoding Method dialog box, select Maximum Quality. Click Finish. The combined image is saved with a new name.

Lesson: Saving Images

Overview

In this lesson you learn how to save images in various ways. In a drawing, images are stored as references linked to the drawing file, not as actual drawing objects. You can save changes to a raster image file without saving the associated vector drawing file.

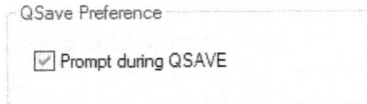

QSave Preference

☑ Prompt during QSAVE

Objectives

After completing this lesson, you will be able to:

- Describe the differences between the Save and Save As commands.
- Determine when to save an image.
- Save a modified image.

Save vs. Save As

You can use the following commands in the Raster tools tab, in the Insert & Write panel, to save the images:

Command	Description
Save	Saves the image file using the original name, location, and file format. This does not change or save the current drawing file.
Save As	Creates a new image file enabling you to select a new name, location, and/or file format. This changes but does not save the current drawing so that it references the new image file.

Using Save

- Use the Save command in the Raster tools tab, in the Insert & Write panel, to save the current image file. All of the drawings referencing the same image file reflect the changes.
- If you save the image file using the Save command, you do not need to save the drawing file separately.
- You can save multiple images at the same time.

Using Save As

- Use the Save As command in the Raster tools tab, in the Insert & Write panel, to save the changes in a new image file. Drawings referencing the original image file do not reflect the changes.
- If you save the image file using this command, you should save the drawing file separately.
- You can only save one image at a time using this command.
- The new image file information displays in the Image tab in the Image Manager (in the Raster tools tab, in the Manage & View panel, click Manage...).

Troubleshooting Saving Images

If you are having problems saving your images, check the following:

- Ensure that the image is not read-only.
- Verify that the path is correct.
- If it is a new image, you need to use the Save As command to give it a name, location, and file format.

Example

You are using an aerial photograph as a background in several drawings, but the original scan is too dark. If you adjust the brightness and contrast and save the changes back to the original file using the Save command. All, all of the drawings using the same image are updated.

You would not use the Save As command, because the changes you made to the image would only be displayed in the current drawing.

When to Save an Image

When you modify an image, you must save the changes back to an image file. Changes can be as simple as adjusting the brightness and contrast using the Histogram command, or as complex as raster entity manipulation (REM). Since image files are not saved during the Autosave process, you must remember to save your changes on a regular basis.

However, several actions trigger a prompt that you have modified an image and it needs to be saved:

- Closing the current drawing.
- Exiting the AutoCAD software.
- Using the AutoCAD Qsave command (default).

Modified Image Options

In the Save Image dialog box (shown in the following illustration), when you are prompted to take action on a modified image, you can use the following options:

Option	Description
Save	Saves the specified image using the same path, name, and format and continues the command.
Save As	Saves the specified image to another path, name, and/or file format.
Save All	Completes the command and saves all images without further prompts.
Skip	Continues the command without saving the specified image.
Skip All	Completes the command without saving any more images.
Information	Displays information about the image, enabling you to determine which action to take.

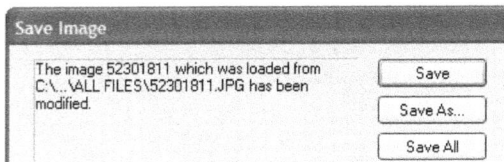

Using the AutoCAD Qsave Command

By default, the AutoCAD Raster Design software prompts you to save any modified images when you use the AutoCAD Qsave command. You can toggle off these prompts using the following steps:

1. In the Raster Tools tab, click the Options arrow in the lower right corner of one of the panels to open the AutoCAD Raster Design Options dialog box.

2. Click the User Preferences tab.

3. Under QSave Preference, clear the Prompt during QSAVE check box as shown in the following illustration.

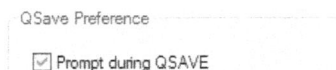

Exercise: Save a Modified Image

In this exercise, you will modify and save a raster image without saving the drawing file.

Name	Status	Saved Path	Active Path
407-Mod	Loaded	407-Mod.tif	C:\AutoCAD Raster Design
407B	Loaded	407B.TIF	C:\AutoCAD Raster Design

The completed exercise

1. Open ...\Saving Images\407.dwg. It has two images placed adjacent to each other.

2. Press SHIFT and click the image on the top left. Note that the grips display.

3. In the Image contextual tab, in the Adjust panel, change the values for Brightness, Contrast, and Fade. The image adjusts as you change the values.

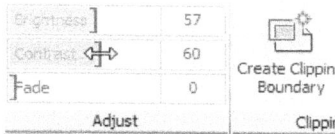

Brightness	57	
Contrast	60	Create Clippin Boundary
Fade	0	
Adjust		Clippir

4. Right-click on the selected image. Click Image>Write>Save As.

5. In the Save As dialog box, rename the image:

    ▪ For File name, enter **407-Mod**.
    ▪ For Files of type, verify that Tagged Image File Format (*.tif, *.tiff) is selected.
    ▪ Click Save.

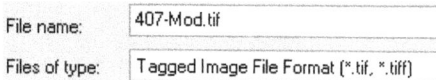

File name:	407-Mod.tif
Files of type:	Tagged Image File Format (*.tif, *.tiff)

6. In the Encoding Method dialog box, verify that Uncompressed is selected.

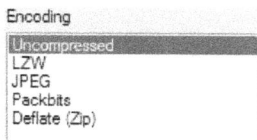

Encoding
```
Uncompressed
LZW
JPEG
Packbits
Deflate (Zip)
```

    ▪ Click Next.

7. In the Data Organization dialog box, select Tiled. Click Finish.

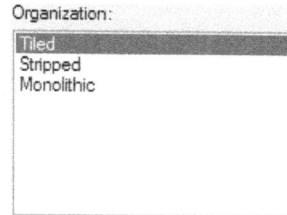

Organization:
```
Tiled
Stripped
Monolithic
```

8. In the Raster Tools tab, in the Manage & View panel, click Manage to open the Image Manager.

9. Switch to the Image Data view by selecting it in the drop-down list. Click 407. The attached images are listed as 407-Mod.tif and 407B.tif in the Images tab.

Name	Status	Saved Path	Active Path
407-Mod	Loaded	407-Mod.tif	C:\AutoCAD Raster Design
407B	Loaded	407B.TIF	C:\AutoCAD Raster Design

Lesson: Exporting Image Files

Overview

In this lesson you learn how to export images and their correlation data. You can export image information when you need to save it without affecting the images inserted in the current drawing. This enables you to convert the file from one format to another and to save correlation data in the image file or as an external correlation file.

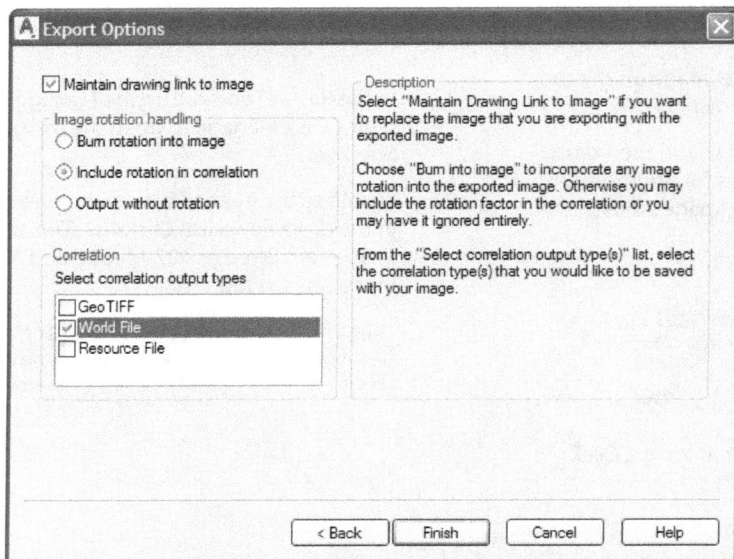

Although there are other ways to save a raster image with a new name and file format, exporting images provides the most flexibility when saving.

Objectives

After completing this lesson, you will be able to:

- Define the terms used when exporting images.
- Determine when it is appropriate to export correlation files.
- Export an image.

Exporting Images and Correlation Files

Although the process of exporting images is similar to that used in saving them, the differences include how correlation information is saved. The correlation file formats that you can save when an image is exported are described in the following sections.

World File

A world file stores the correlation information for an image. It is an ASCII file that you can view using Notepad. Most mapping software require world files. By default, these files are saved in the folder in which the image is located. World files are created (and searched for on insert) with different extensions, depending on the file format. Note that all of these file formats end in the letter W, indicating that these are world files.

Resource File

A resource file is used by the AutoCAD Raster Design software to store image correlation data, such as insertion point, scale, and rotation. Once saved, it can be used as a source of correlation information when an image is inserted into a drawing. Resource files have the same base name as the raster image, but use an *.RES* extension.

Export Options

The following options are supported when exporting an image:

Option	Description
Maintain drawing link to image	Inserts the new image file in place of the original being exported. The result is similar to using the Save As command.
Burn rotation into image	Permanently realigns the image to match the current rotation angle.
Include rotation in correlation	Saves the image with its current rotation.
Output without rotation	Saves the image without its current rotation.

Example

You have created an image that is going to be used as the background for several drawings in a project. The image needs to be saved with its coordinate information, so that it displays in the correct location when inserted into the various drawings. This can be done using the Export command to create a resource file.

When to Use Correlation Files

The Export command can save different types of correlation files. Each of these file formats can be applied to different situations. The following guidelines can be used to help determine which correlation file works best in different situations.

Guidelines

Note the following when exporting correlation data:

- Resource files are meant to be used with images inserted using the AutoCAD Raster Design software.
- World files can be used with mapping, GIS, and other image management software.
- You can export a world file without exporting the image file.
- When saving external correlation files, ensure that their paths are saved correctly.

Additionally, the Export options can be used to save the correlation data in the image file header.

Example

You are cleaning up several images to use as the background for a large mapping or GIS database. After you locate and edit the images, you can export their correlation data as world files for use in your mapping or GIS software.

You would not use the Save As command because it does not provide options for saving external correlation files, which are available when using the Export options.

Exercise: Export an Image

In this exercise, you will export an image and save the associated correlation data.

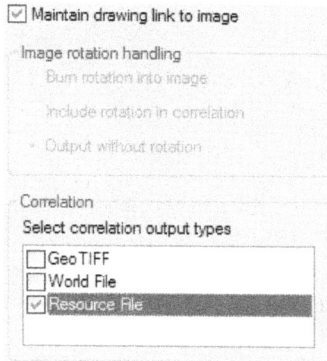

The completed exercise

1. Open ...\Exporting Images\Ind_Park.dwg.

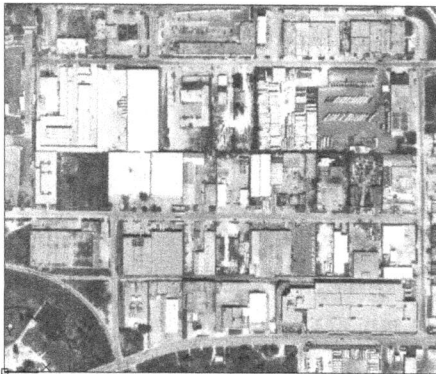

2. Select and right-click on the edge of the image. Click Image>Write>Export.

3. In the Export dialog box, for Files of type, select Tagged Image File Format (*.tif, *.tiff).

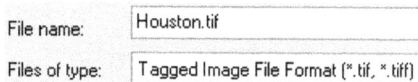

| File name: | Houston.tif |
| Files of type: | Tagged Image File Format (*.tif, *.tiff) |

4. Click Export.

5. In the Encoding Method dialog box, verify that Uncompressed is selected.

6. Click Next.

7. In the Data Organization dialog box, select Tiled.

8. Click Next.

9. In the Export Options dialog box, specify the correlation output type:
   - Select the Maintain drawing link to image check box.
   - Under Select correlation output types, select Resource File.

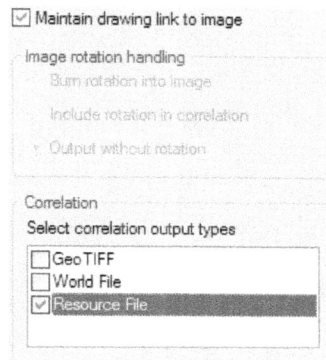

10. Click Finish.

Chapter Summary

Having completed this chapter, you can:

- Work with tiled images.
- Save images.
- Export image files.

Working with Multispectral Images

This chapter introduces you to working with multispectral images, including how to insert them into a drawing and how to analyze them. These images are often used for large-scale mapping and planning projects.

Objectives

After completing this chapter, you will be able to:

- Insert multispectral images.
- Analyze multispectral images.

Lesson: Inserting and Analyzing Multispectral Images

Overview

In this lesson you learn how to incorporate multispectral imagery into a drawing. A multispectral image is similar to an expanded version of a typical RGB color image, in which several color bands represent different data types that can be collated to form an image.

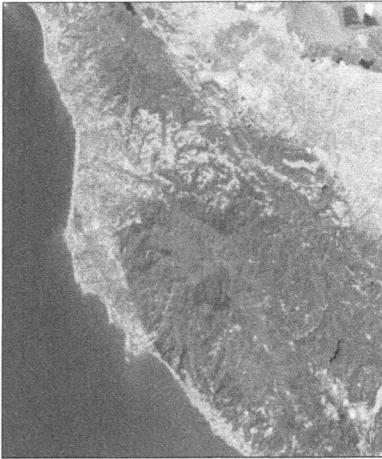

Data that represents information that is not usually displayed in visible light photographs, such as temperature or ultraviolet data, can be visualized in a multispectral image.

Objectives

After completing this lesson, you will be able to:

- Identify the types and sources of multispectral imagery.
- Define the terms color band and band assignment color map.
- Determine when multispectral imagery is required.
- Identify and gather different types of data that can be incorporated into a multispectral image.
- Insert a multispectral image.
- Change a band assignment color map.

About Multispectral Images

Visualizing Data

Before the introduction of multispectral images, you could only use images as backgrounds in AutoCAD® drawings. They could represent different types of data, but were static pictures. Now you have a powerful tool for analyzing different data types and noting how they interact with each other.

Several images, each representing a different element of a site, can be combined in many ways to create a full portrait of an area.

An area in true color is shown in the following illustration.

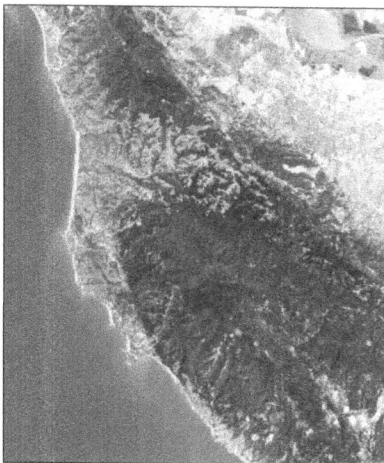

The same area in false color, where the red colors represent the area as seen in the infrared, is shown in the following illustration.

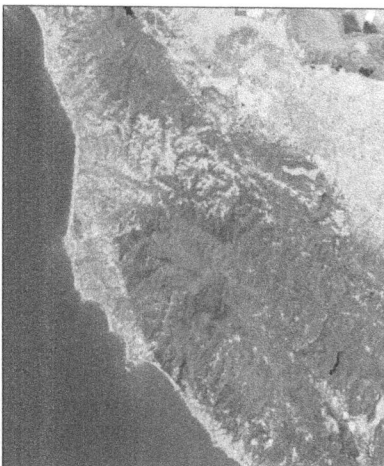

Multispectral Images

Each band of a multispectral image set is an image from a different segment of the full electromagnetic spectrum, of which the visible bands (red, green, and blue) are only a part. By channeling a specific combination of images to the Red, Green, and Blue colors used to display a picture on the computer, you can display very specific characteristics of the land.

Three images of the same area, each taken in a different wavelength are shown in the following illustration.

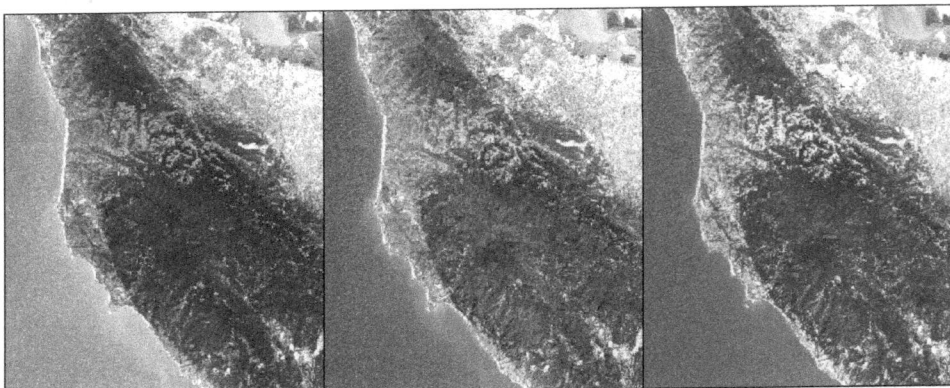

The same three images combined into a single multispectral image are shown in the following illustration.

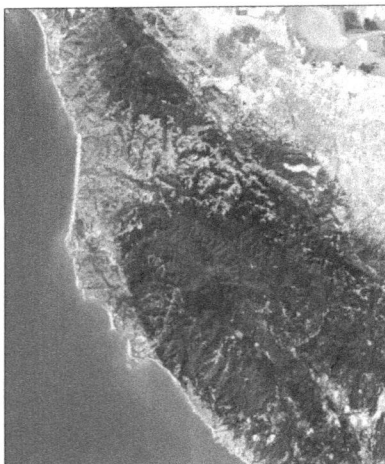

GeoTIFF

GeoTIFF is a standard for storing georeference and geocoding information in a raster file that is TIFF 6.0 compliant. Georeferencing ties the pixels in an image to a reference location that might not be tied to a location on the earth. Geocoding uses an algorithm to precisely determine the location on earth for each point in the image.

The information that is written into the raster file sizes and locates the image correctly on the earth. Most satellite images are available as GeoTIFFs.

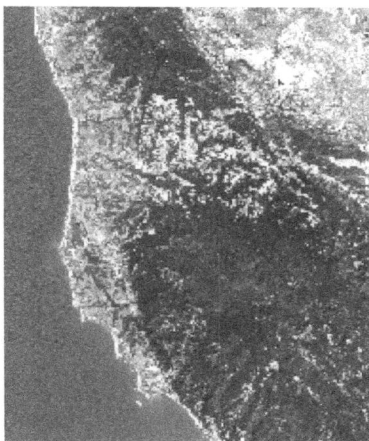

Requirements

Source images used to create a multispectral image must meet the following conditions:

- Each image must represent a separate segment of the electromagnetic spectrum.
- Each image must be in the GeoTIFF format.
- Each image must be georeferenced using the same coordinate system.

Example

Multispectral images combine various types of data about the same area into one coherent picture. They are not used to combine images of different areas into one image.

In the following illustration, color bands for infrared, visible green, and blue are combined to create a false color image. Vegetation displays in shades of red, while the surrounding water is blue. The different shades of red represent the various types and health of the vegetation in this area.

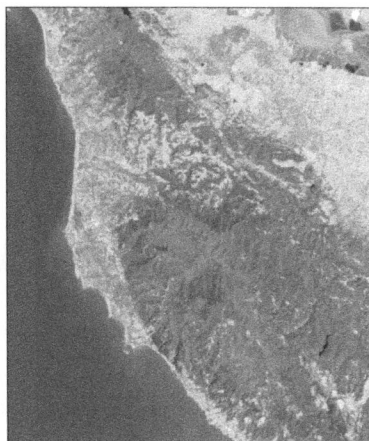

Understanding Color Bands and Band Assignments

Color Band

Data used in a multispectral image is recorded in the form of multiple bands. Each band records the values in a specific range of the spectrum, such as infrared, visible, or ultraviolet. Data gathered by satellites is typically provided in the multispectral format.

Band Assignment Color Map

A band assignment color map selects the data bands to display and assigns each band to a color channel (Red, Blue, or Green). You can use this to create false color images from individual color bands.

☑ Red:	B30 <L71044034_03419990707_b30.tif> ⌄
☑ Green:	B20 <L71044034_03419990707_b20.tif> ⌄
☑ Blue:	B10 <L71044034_03419990707_b10.tif> ⌄

☑ Insert into display

Changing the Band Assignment Color Map

If you have many different color bands associated with the same multispectral image, you might sometimes need to change which color bands display. For example, if you are analyzing ocean surface temperature ranges, you might have more than three color bands. The band assignment color map controls this display.

☑ Red:	B40 <L71044034_03419990707_b40.tif> ⌄
☑ Green:	B30 <L71044034_03419990707_b30.tif> ⌄
☑ Blue:	B20 <L71044034_03419990707_b20.tif> ⌄

Considerations When Working with Color Bands

When you work with color bands, note the following:

- Each color band is an image that is stored as a separate file.
- You must have a minimum of two color bands to create a multispectral image.
- Not all combinations yield images that can be interpreted clearly.

Example

In the first pair of images, visible red, green, and blue images have been combined to form a natural color image of the area.

The band assignment color map is shown in the following illustration.

☑ Red:	B30 <L71044034_03419990707_b30.tif> ⌄
☑ Green:	B20 <L71044034_03419990707_b20.tif> ⌄
☑ Blue:	B10 <L71044034_03419990707_b10.tif> ⌄

The resulting natural color image is shown in the following illustration.

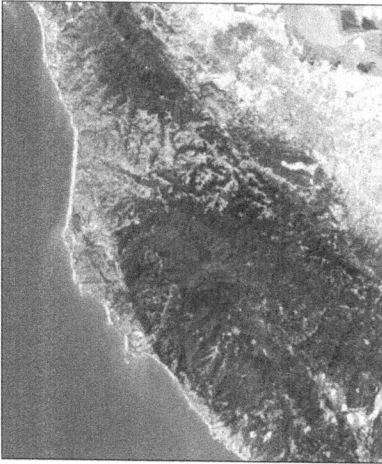

In this second set of images, the band assignment color map is changed to display a false color image in which infrared has been substituted for visible red.

The revised band assignment color map is shown in the following illustration.

The resulting false color image is shown in the following illustration.

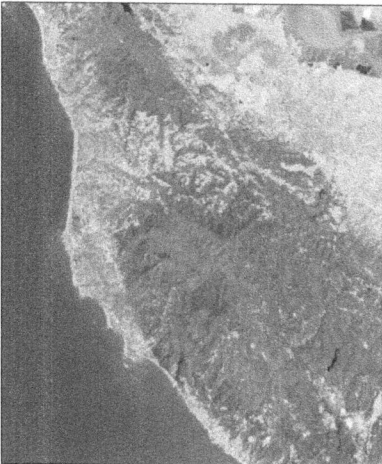

When to Use Multispectral Images

Determining whether your use of multispectral images is going to be effective, depends on the available data and what you are trying to accomplish. Not all data can or should be used to form a multispectral image. For example, if the information in each color band is too similar, the resulting multispectral image looks very similar to the separate color bands, offering no new information.

Use the following guidelines to determine whether the available data can create a relevant and useful multispectral image, and for suggestions about the different types of multispectral images:

- At least two color bands displaying variability must be available.
- You can use many color bands in the same image and change the band assignment color map to analyze different combinations of the data.
- Each color band should display the same physical area.
- Several multispectral images can be created from color bands taken at different times to indicate changes in an area over time.
- Not all combinations of color bands produce useful information.

Example

The images shown in the following illustration display data from a meteorological satellite in infrared and visible wavelengths. High, cirrus clouds display brightly in the infrared as shown on the left, but poorly in visible light as shown on the right. Lower clouds display more clearly in visible light.

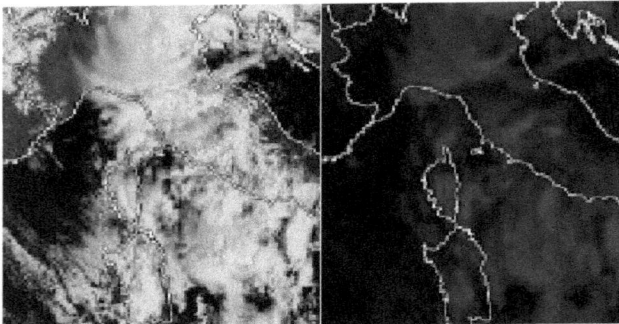

The image shown in the following illustration collates the data into a multispectral image that displays the full distribution of cloud cover and any variations in cloud patterns at different elevations.

Preparing to Use Multispectral Images

Before you can create a multispectral image, you must collect the color bands and set up a drawing. You should also have a good idea of the type of analysis you are trying to create.

Name	Date m
L71044034_03419990707_b10.tif	1/20/20
L71044034_03419990707_b20.tif	1/20/20
L71044034_03419990707_b30.tif	1/20/20
L71044034_03419990707_b40.tif	1/20/20
L71044034_03419990707_b50.tif	1/20/20
L71044034_03419990707_b61.tif	1/20/20
L72044034_03419990707_b62.tif	1/20/20
L72044034_03419990707_b70.tif	1/20/20
L72044034_03419990707_b80.tif	1/20/20

Creating a Multispectral Image

To create a multispectral image, you need to insert all of the images that represent the individual color bands at the same time. In the Insert Image dialog box, under Insert Options, you can select the Treat as multispectral check box to aggregate these images into a single multispectral image.

Insert Options

○ Quick insert   ☐ Show frames only

⦿ Insertion wizard   ☐ Zoom to image(s)

○ Insertion dialog   ☑ Treat as multispectral

Multispectral Image Setup

When you are creating several multispectral images to analyze the spread of urban development over time for a specific area, you need to do the following:

- Collect the images that are going to represent the color bands used for the multispectral image.
- Set up the drawing that you are going to use to analyze the multispectral image to display the same area.

Guidelines for Creating a Multispectral Image

When you create a multispectral image, note the following:

- Sources for color band images include most satellite data, such as Landsat or GOES-8 meteorological data.
- Each image must be a separate color band and georeferenced and geocoded for the same area.
- Your data must be organized so that if you are creating several multispectral images, you can identify the color bands that are going to be used for each image.

Guidelines for Inserting Multispectral Images

When you insert color band images, note the following:

- Insert all of the images representing the color bands at the same time.
- Select the Treat As Multispectral check box.

Exercise: Insert a Multispectral Image

In this exercise, you will select several images to use as color bands for a multispectral image. You then select the color bands to display using the Image Insertion wizard.

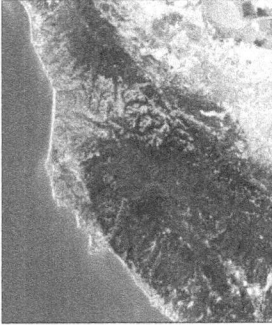

The completed exercise

1. Open ...\Inserting and Analyzing Multispectral Images\multi_spec_1.dwg.

2. In the Raster Tools tab, in the Insert & Write panel, click Insert.

3. In the Insert Image dialog box, set the path to ...\Inserting and Analyzing Multispectral Images. Click L71044034_03419990707_b10.tif, press and hold SHIFT, and click L72044034_03419990707_b80.tif so that all of the images in the list are highlighted.

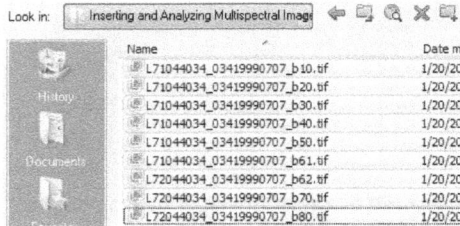

4. Under Insert Options, verify that Insertion wizard is selected. Select Treat as multispectral and clear Zoom to image(s).

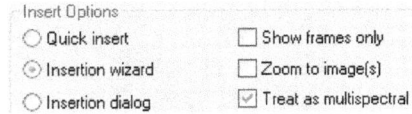

- Click Open.

5. Select the check boxes for all three color bands, Red, Green, and Blue, if required. Select the Insert into display check box.

6. For Red, in the list, select L71044034_03419990707_b30.tif. For Green, select L71044034_03419990707_b20.tif. For Blue, select L71044034_03419990707_b10.tif.

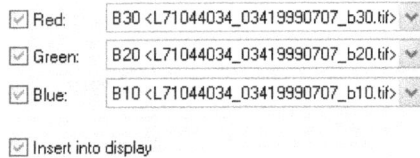

7. Click Next for each page of the Image Insertion wizard. Click Finish on the last page of the wizard. Zoom to the extents of the drawing.

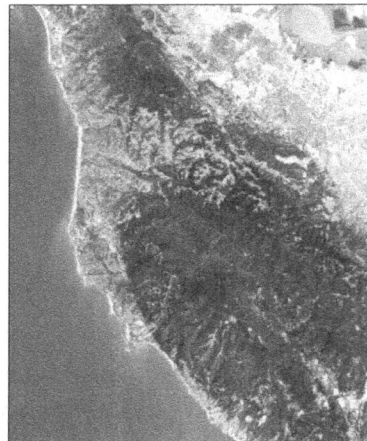

Exercise: Change a Band Assignment Color Map

In this exercise, you will change the color bands displayed in an existing multispectral image.

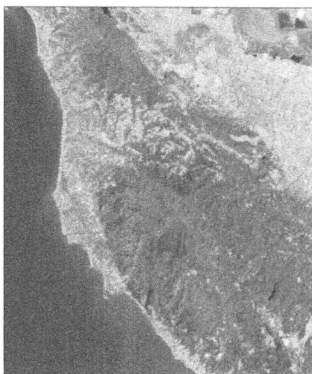

The completed exercise

1. Open ...\Inserting and Analyzing Multispectral Images\multi_spec_2.dwg.

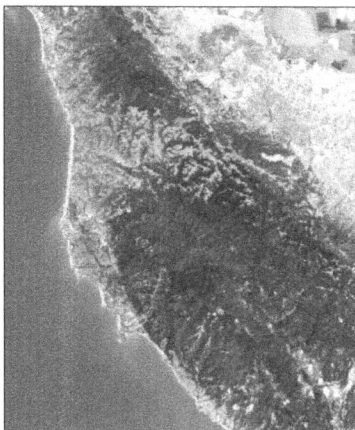

2. In the Raster Tools tab, in the Manage & View panel, click Manage.

3. In the View list, click Image Insertions.

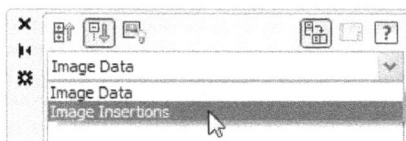

4. Expand the *multi_spec_2* tree. Right-click on *L72044034_03419990707*. Click Edit Color Map.

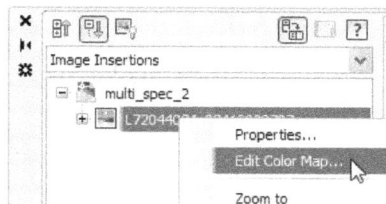

5. In the Band Assignment Color Map dialog box, for Red, select *L71044034_03419990707_b40.tif*. For Green, select *L71044034_03419990707_b30.tif*. For Blue, select *L71044034_03419990707_b20.tif*.

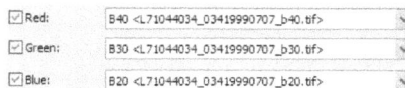

- Click OK.

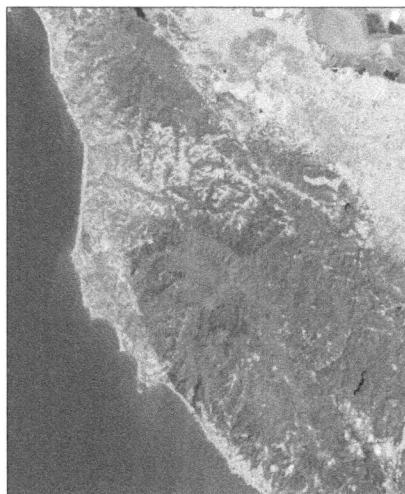

Chapter Summary

Having completed this chapter, you can:

- Insert multispectral images.
- Analyze multispectral images.

Correlating and Rubbersheeting Images

This chapter introduces several tools that you can use to correlate an image after you have inserted it into an AutoCAD® drawing. These include both linear and nonlinear methods for matching the image to the coordinate system of the drawing.

Objectives

After completing this chapter, you will be able to:

- Correlate scanned drawings.
- Rubbersheet images.

Lesson: Correlating Scanned Drawings

Overview

In this lesson you learn how to use the AutoCAD® Raster Design tools that enable you to create a linear correlation. Although you can correlate an image at the time of its insertion, not all images have obvious correlation data, including location, scale, and orientation. The AutoCAD Raster Design software contains tools that correlate images after they have been inserted into a drawing.

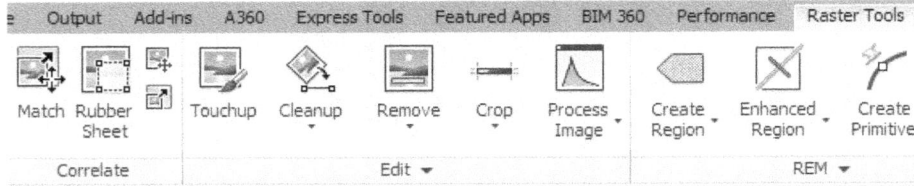

Objectives

After completing this lesson, you will be able to:

- Define raster image correlation.
- Decide when to use linear correlation tools.
- Move or displace an image.
- Scale an image.
- Match an image to vectors.

About Correlation

Correlation is the use of information about an image (including insertion point, rotation, and scale), to match it to a drawing.

Linear Correlation Defined

Linear correlation modifies the entire image as a single object without distorting the image. This type of correlation regulates the image's position, size, and rotation.

The effect of linear correlation on raster images is the same as that of using editing commands, such as Move, Scale, and Rotate, on vector entities.

Key Terms

In addition to the main correlation definitions, the following terms are useful.

Term	Definition
Insertion Point	The insertion point incorporates the X, Y, and Z coordinates where the image is located. It is based on the lower-left corner of the image.
Scale	The scale is used to resize an image based on its original size. For example, a scale of 2 makes the image twice as large in the drawing as it was in the original image file.
Rotation	Rotation is the angle at which an image is revolved about its insertion point.
Orthorectified Image	When an image is corrected so that all pixels represent their true locations on the face of the Earth, it is called an orthorectified image. This process makes directions and distances accurate in the image. All distortions resulting from parallax, lens distortion, and other causes are removed.

Example

You are working on a large development project with grading plans that are printed across several sheets. After scanning them, you want to tile them together to display the entire project. When you have inserted one image, you can use the correlation tools to match the rest of the images to the insertion point, scale, and rotation angle of the first image.

You would not use these correlation tools to match existing vectors to your raster image. Raster images tend to be less accurate than correctly drawn vector information.

Which Correlation Tools To Use

The AutoCAD Modify and AutoCAD Raster Design linear correlation commands are tools that you can use to correlate an image. Each tool is appropriate for different editing conditions. This section helps you to determine which tools are best for your projects.

> You can use correlation tools from both categories on the same image. For example, you can use the AutoCAD Move command to place an image in roughly the correct location, and then use the AutoCAD Raster Design Match command to refine the location, size, and orientation of the image.

AutoCAD Modify Commands

The commands in the AutoCAD Home tab, in the Modify panel are best used in the following situations:

- You have a single image that you want to move or rotate, but no specific targets, such as vectors or other images.
- You only need to change the frame, not the contents, of the image itself.
- You need to perform a single, simple operation, such as rotating the image 90 degrees.

The Modify commands in the AutoCAD Home tab, in the Modify panel are shown in the following illustration.

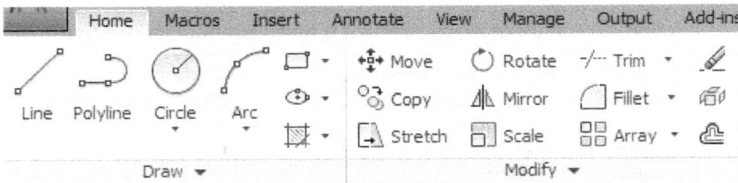

Linear Correlation Tools

The AutoCAD Raster Design software contains several tools that you can use to perform linear correlations. These commands are located in the Raster Tools tab, in the Correlate panel, and can be used on any image type.

Although some of these commands duplicate the effects of the AutoCAD editing commands, they provide more options and image-specific selection methods, such as SHIFT + click.

Command	Description
Displace	Changes the position of an image or moves it.
Scale	Resizes an image proportionally.
Match	Rotates, resizes, and moves an image based on two reference points.

Linear Correlation Guidelines

The AutoCAD Raster Design linear correlation commands are best used in the following situations:

- You are trying to match two images to each other for tiling into a larger, composite image.
- Two images were saved with different base-unit systems.
- You are matching an orthorectified image to an existing set of vectors.
- You are working with paper plans that were scanned with little or no distortion.

The correlation tools in the AutoCAD Raster Design software are shown in the following illustration.

Example

You want to use an orthorectified aerial photograph as a background for a proposed development. You can use the Match command to select two points on the photograph and match them to features in the design.

Exercise: Move or Displace an Image

In this exercise, you will use the Displace command to change the position of an image by moving it by a required offset. Displacing moves an image without rotating or scaling it, so that a base point on the image matches a destination point on an existing vector entity or raster image.

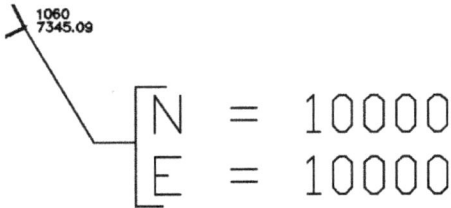

1060
7345.09

$$N = 10000$$
$$E = 10000$$

10000.93, 10000.29, 0.00   MODEL

The completed exercise

1. Open ...\Correlating Scanned Drawings\ PropSite.dwg.

2. Zoom to the lower-right corner of the drawing.

1060
7345.09

$$N = 10000$$
$$E = 10000$$

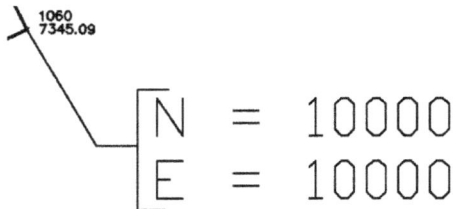

3. Point 1060 in the image is a control point with coordinates 10000,10000. Hover the cursor over the point and note the coordinates in the Status Bar. The actual location of this point is around 16040,3340 in the drawing because the image coordinate system does not match the drawing coordinate system. Therefore, you must displace the image.

16040.28, 3340.14, 0.00   MODEL

4. In the Raster Tools tab, in the Correlate panel, click Displace.

5. Displace the image:
   - Select the intersection of the lines at point 1060 as the base point.
   - Enter **-6040, 6660** as an offset distance for the destination point for the image.

6. Zoom to the extents of the image.

7. Zoom in close to point 1060.

1060
7345.09

$$N = 10000$$
$$E = 10000$$

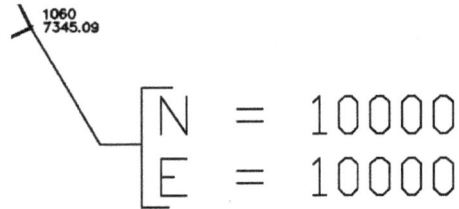

Hover the cursor over the intersection point, note that the image coordinates are similar to the survey coordinates.

10000.93, 10000.29, 0.00   MODEL

Exercise: Scale an Image

You can scale a raster image so that it matches elements in a vector drawing or another image, or so that elements in the image are 1:1 (life-size). In this exercise, you will scale an existing raster image.

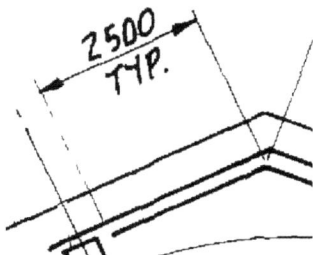

```
Distance = 2499.6833,   Angle in X
Delta X = 2263.3785,   Delta Y = 1
```

The completed exercise

1. Open ...\Correlating Scanned Drawings\ Site1.dwg.

2. Zoom in to the 2500 TYP. dimension at the top of the plan.

3. Check the distance:
   - Enter **DI** to start the DIST command.
   - Pick the end of the left dimension arrow as the first point.
   - Pick the end of the right dimension arrow as the second point.

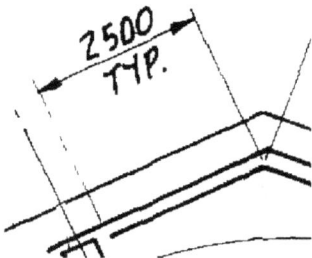

4. Note that the distance between the two points displays along with the cursor and also in the Command Line.

```
Distance = 25.1062,   Angle
Delta X = 22.6412,   Delta Y
```

Although the dimension on the image indicates that the distance is 2500, the actual distance displays around 25 because of the scale of the image.

5. In the Raster Tools tab, in the Correlate panel, click Scale.

6. Specify the Scale settings:
   - Enter **0,0** as the base point.
   - Pick the end of the left dimension arrow and the right dimension arrow as the source distance.
   - Enter **2500** as the destination distance.

7. Zoom to the extents of the image.

8. Zoom back in to the 2500 TYP. dimension that you just scaled.

9. Check the distance:
   - Enter **DI** to start the DIST command.
   - Pick the end of the left dimension arrow as the first point.
   - Pick the end of the right dimension arrow as the second point.

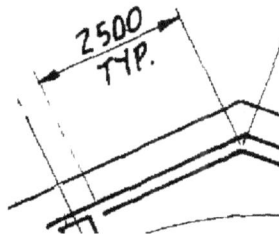

10. Note that the corrected distance between the two points displays along with the cursor.

```
Distance = 2499.6833,   Angle in X
Delta X = 2263.3785,   Delta Y = 1
```

Exercise: Match an Image to Vectors

You can change the image size and alignment by matching two points on it with two known points on a drawing. In this exercise, you will match a raster image to a vector drawing.

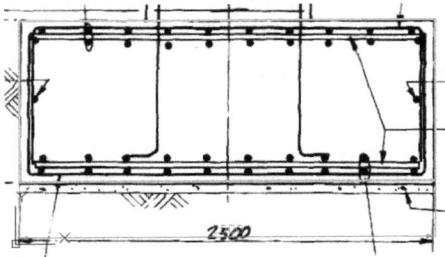

The completed exercise

1. Open ...\Correlating Scanned Drawings\ Section-A.dwg.

2. In the Raster Tools tab, in the Correlate panel, click Match.

3. Match the raster lines to the vector lines in the left viewport:

   - Specify source point #1 by picking the lower-left corner of the raster foundation just above the image dimension line.
   - Specify destination point #1 by picking the intersection of the green vector lines.

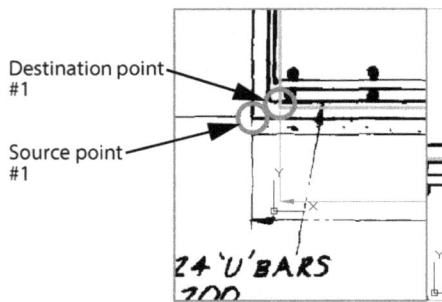

4. Match the raster lines to the vector lines in the right viewport:

   - Activate the right viewport by clicking anywhere.
   - Pick the corner of the raster foundation as source point #2.
   - Pick the intersection of the green vector lines as destination point #2.

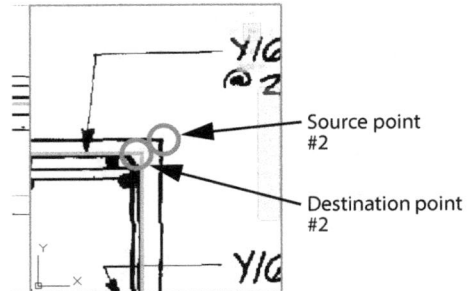

5. Verify that the raster lines on the image now match the vector lines in the drawing.

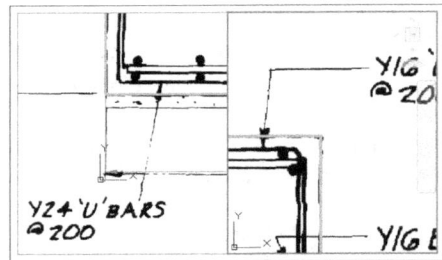

6. Click the Model tab at the bottom of the screen.

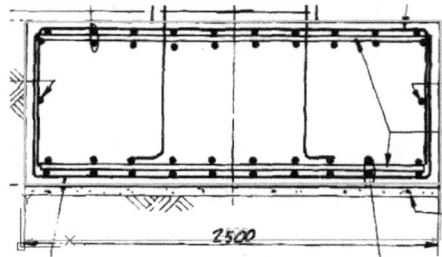

The corrected image displays.

Lesson: Rubbersheeting Images

Overview

Rubbersheet is an advanced correlation tool. In this lesson you learn how to use the features of the Rubbersheet command to stretch images to accurately match selected control points in a drawing.

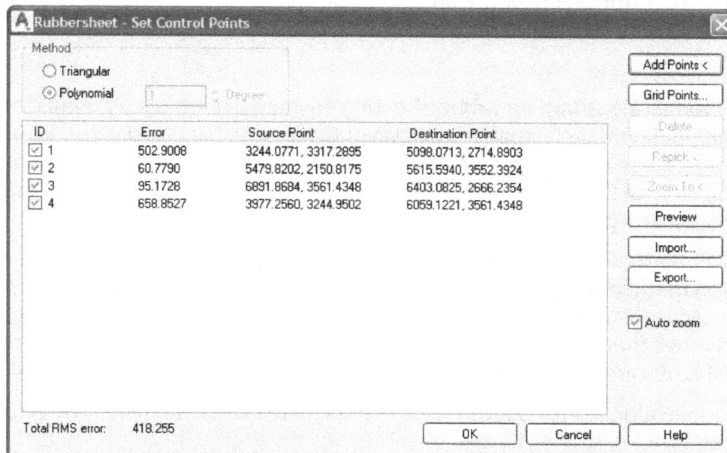

Raster images rarely match existing vectors or other images that are imported into a drawing. Rubbersheeting is the only means by which you can accurately warp the image to match the vectors more closely.

Objectives

After completing this lesson, you will be able to:

- Define the terms used when rubbersheeting images.
- Describe the different rubbersheeting methods.
- Identify the different methods for specifying control points.
- Determine when rubbersheeting an image is appropriate.
- Explain the process of rubbersheeting.
- Rubbersheet an image.

About Rubbersheeting

Rubbersheeting is a correlation process that largely removes any distortions in an image. You define sets of control points in the image that warp it and the software then stretches the image as if it were printed on a sheet of rubber, based on the selected points. All of the standard image types can be rubbersheeted.

Using AutoCAD commands and basic correlation tools, you can scale and rotate the image as a whole, but cannot modify the internal distribution of the pixels in the image. Using the Rubbersheet command, you have more control over how the image can be modified.

Root Mean Square Error

When you use the polynomial algorithm for rubbersheeting an image, there is a difference between the selected destination point and the actual destination of the image. These individual errors are reported when you display the selected control points and displayed when you preview an image. The root mean square (RMS) error of the rubbersheeting process is a value that provides an overall total error for the entire set of control points.

The RMS error is calculated by taking the square root of the sum of all of the valid control point errors. Note that this calculation method gives greater weight to larger individual errors. A single control point with a large error can result in a much greater RMS error for the control point set. Control points can be toggled off to remove them from the RMS error calculation and the rubbersheeting process. However, the individual errors are still reported for checking purposes.

When you use the triangular algorithm, no RMS errors are calculated because there is no error at the individual control points.

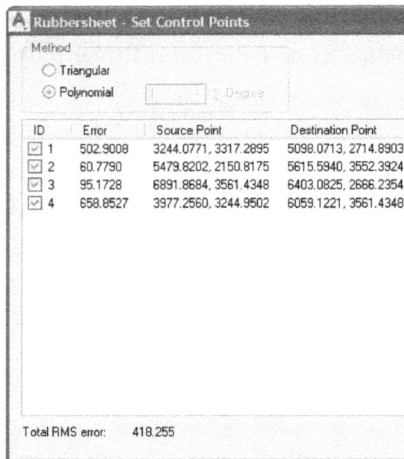

Example

You are matching a scanned tax map to a set of property lines that were drawn as vectors. However, either the tax map was not drawn to scale or the media on which it was printed stretched during the scanning process. The errors you encounter in this case are nonlinear. Therefore, you need to use rubbersheeting to remove them. You cannot use the basic correlation tools because the errors vary in different areas of the map.

Rubbersheeting Methods

The two algorithms used to rubbersheet an image are polynomial and triangular. Each method affects the image in a different way.

Polynomial Algorithm

The polynomial rubbersheeting algorithm uses a single formula across the entire image for the stretching process. Depending on the location of the control points, the distance each location is changed, and the selected polynomial degree, the image might be warped dramatically. Additionally, since a single formula is used, it is rare that all of the locations match their selected destinations exactly. There are usually some RMS errors.

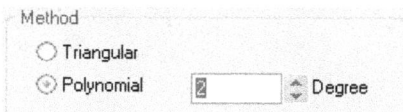

Method
- ○ Triangular
- ◉ Polynomial ⬚ 2 ⬚ ⬍ Degree

Polynomial Degree

The polynomial degree controls the exact formula used to calculate the new locations in a rubbersheeted image. When you select a greater number of control points, a higher polynomial degree is available. The increased degree applies a higher function to the rubbersheeting process, but results in a greater amount of distortion to the original image. You can use a lower polynomial degree if required.

The simplest analogy to the polynomial degree is how best-fit curves can be applied to points. If you have two points, you can draw a straight line that touches both points. If you have three points, you might not be able to draw a straight line touching all three points. However, you could draw an arc between the three points. The arc would represent a higher function than the line and is a more complex shape.

Triangular Algorithm

The triangular rubbersheeting algorithm calculates the amount of change in a piecewise fashion for each triangular region between three control points. This algorithm guarantees that each location matches its destination exactly when the rubbersheeting is finished. Since the triangular algorithm only works between control points, any portions of the image outside the control points are removed. When using this algorithm, ensure that control points are set for all portions of the image that you want to keep.

Method
- ◉ Triangular
- ○ Polynomial ⬚ 2 ⬚ ⬍ Degree

Example

You want to exactly match the buildings in an aerial photograph to the vector footprints of those buildings in a drawing. You use the triangular algorithm because it gives an exact match to the selected control points. When you have finished rubbersheeting, you crop the image around the outside of the rubbersheeted area because it has an irregular border.

About Control Points

All of the rubbersheeting methods rely on the selection of control points to determine how the image is stretched. A control point is actually a pair of points that define locations in the raster image and the required destination for that location. They are sometimes called the "from" and "to" points.

ID	Error	Source Point	Destination Point
☑ 1	65.7683	9659.0791, 17897.3711	9531.6798, 17981.7811
☑ 2	127.30	8902.9466, 15034.2193	8902.9466, 15034.2193

Control Point List

Sets of control points can be written out to an external ASCII file. This file can be imported for use with another image, or to recorrelate the same image using a different algorithm or polynomial degree.

File name:	sub_aerial_1
Files of type:	Point Files (*.txt)

Control Point Grid

You can set up a control point grid when you match an image using points that are regularly spaced. This is very useful when grid lines on USGS maps or structural designs are present. The software sets up a regular grid based on your parameters for the destination points. You then step through this grid to specify the source points in the raster image to match to the grid.

Grid Parameters

Points	Grid	Cell
Rows:	X Origin:	X Size:
5	1172.584	1.000
Columns:	Y Origin:	Y Size:
5	1042.916	1.000
Total:	Pick <	Pick <
25		

Preview   Add Points <   Cancel   Help

Example

You need to use a single set of control points to match an image to the foreground vectors, and you have to try several different methods of rubbersheeting to get the required results. Rather than reselecting the points each time, you can export the control points from one attempt and import the control point list for subsequent attempts.

Guidelines for Rubbersheeting

The tools used to adjust the scale of an image cannot apply different scaling factors over different portions of the image. You might need this enhanced control over how the image is changed, or you might have exact control points, from existing survey data, vector drawings, or measured dimensions. Using the Rubbersheet command, you can apply precise values to the raster image.

- A minimum of three control points is required, although many control points can be selected.
- When processing the image, you can ignore specific control points if the error values are too high.
- When you use the triangular algorithm, the image outside the control points is lost.
- If you rubbersheet an image multiple times (e.g., trying a different algorithm or polynomial degree), you can export the control points so that you can import them for future use.

Example

For the best results, use rubbersheeting when you work with the following types of image:

- Aerial photography, because the attitude of the aircraft, topographic relief of the ground, and lens distortion can affect the quality of the image.
- Scanned blueprints, because both the reproduction method and the scanning process can stretch the media when using roll-feed devices.
- Digital photography, because perspective, camera tilt, and lens distortion can affect the image.
- An image that was not drawn to scale, but needs to be adjusted to match the actual dimensions.

Image Correlation Process

To correlate an image, use the Match and Scale tools to place it in the general location at an approximate scale. You can then use the Rubbersheet command to fit the image more accurately using control points.

Procedure: Applying Rubbersheeting to an Image

For the best results, use the following method:

1. Select the control points.

2. Preview the resulting image.

3. Select or change the control points and preview the resulting image.

4. Repeat this process for all of the required control points.

5. Apply the rubbersheeting.

You can repeat this cycle as many times as required before applying the changes to the image. The preview step identifies areas in which the error is great or the portions of the raster image that might be highly distorted or removed.

Rubbersheeting Tips

The following tips can help you when using rubbersheeting:

- Control points can be toggled on or off, deleted, or reselected using Repick.
- When using the polynomial algorithm, highlight any control point in the list, click Zoom To, and preview the image to graphically display the amount of error generated by the control point.

Exercise: Rubbersheet an Image

In this exercise, you will rubbersheet an image to correct its distortions.

The completed exercise

1. Open ...\Rubbersheeting Images\ subdivision_17.dwg.

2. In the upper-left viewport, press SHIFT + click. In the Image Select dialog box, select sub_aerial. Click OK.

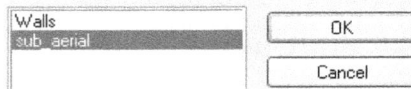

3. In the Raster Tools tab, in the Correlate panel, click Rubber Sheet.

4. Begin the correlation:

   - In the Rubbersheet dialog box, click Add Points.
   - Click the center of the gray plus sign as the source point #1.

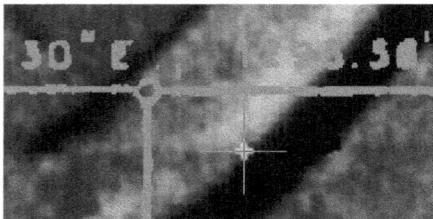

5. Click the center of the red circle that is the property corner as the destination point #1.

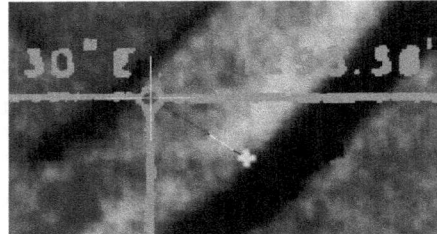

6. Click anywhere in the bottom-left viewport to activate it. Specify the source point #2 by clicking the center of the gray plus sign located between the red circles and partially covered by the red line. For destination point #2, enter **A** to anchor the point.

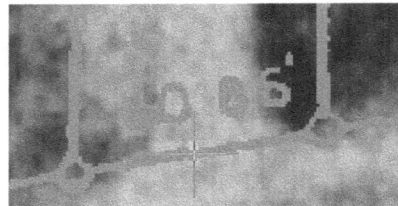

7. Activate the bottom-right viewport and click the center of the gray plus sign as source point #3. Click the center of the red circle as destination point #3.

8. Activate the top-right viewport and click the center of the gray plus sign as source point #4. Click the center of the red circle as destination point #4.

9. Press ENTER. In the Rubbersheet dialog box, note that four ids are added.

ID	Error	Source Point	Destination Point
☑ 1	0.0000...	9658.1040, 17896.1008	9528.8023, 17977.3505
☑ 2	0.0000...	8903.2036, 15031.9184	8903.2036, 15031.9184
☑ 3	0.0000...	15398.4655, 14963.0576	15432.3585, 14863.1104
☑ 4	0.0000...	15313.3942, 17284.4357	15367.5832, 17203.6324

10. In the Rubbersheet dialog box, click Export.

11. In the Export dialog box, click Export.

12. In the Rubbersheet dialog box, click OK to start the rubbersheeting process.

13. Switch to a single viewport (View tab> Model Viewports panel).

14. Zoom extents to display the corrected photo.

15. Click Undo until all of the edits have been completely undone. The Command Line will read "Everything has been undone."

16. In the upper-left viewport, press SHIFT + click. Click sub_aerial. Click OK.

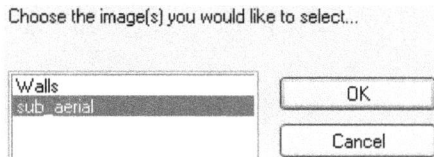

17. In the Raster Tools tab, in the Correlate panel, click Rubbersheet.

18. In the Rubbersheet dialog box, click Import.

19. In the Import dialog box, select *sub_aerial_1.txt*. Click Open.

In the Rubbersheet dialog box, the points that you previously exported to *sub_aerial_1.txt* display.

20. Under Method, click Polynomial.

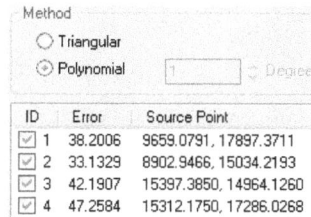

ID	Error	Source Point
1	38.2006	9659.0791, 17897.3711
2	33.1329	8902.9466, 15034.2193
3	42.1907	15397.3850, 14964.1260
4	47.2584	15312.1750, 17286.0268

21. Click OK.

22. Switch to a single viewport.

23. Zoom extents to display the corrected photo.

Chapter Summary

Having completed this chapter, you can:

- Correlate scanned drawings.
- Rubbersheet images.

Enhancing the Appearance of Images

This chapter introduces tools that you can use to clean up the appearance of an image before you plot a raster image. Using them, you can fix errors, such as mirrored or inverted images in scanned black-and-white drawings, and adjust the color balance in true-color photographs.

Objectives

After completing this chapter, you will be able to:

- Fix errors in scanned images.
- Use the bitonal filters.
- Use the convolve filters.
- Work with a histogram.
- Control colors with the Palette Manager.

Lesson: Fixing Errors in Scanned Images

Overview

By using cleanup tools, you can improve the readability of raster images and make changes that apply to an entire image. In this lesson you learn how to use the Deskew, Invert, and Mirror tools to improve the appearance of your raster data. These tools are used to rotate an image in its frame, change colors in an image, or reverse an entire image.

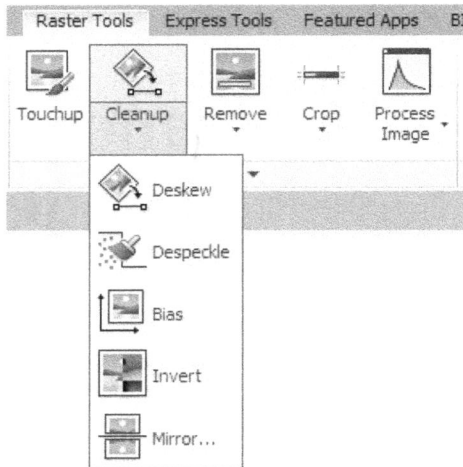

Objectives

After completing this lesson, you will be able to:

- Define the terms used when fixing errors in a scanned document.
- Explain the terms used when inverting and mirroring images.
- Determine which tools to use when fixing errors in a scanned drawing.
- Explain the process of scanning images and editing when required.
- Deskew an image.
- Invert and mirror an image.

About General Cleanup Tools

You can use the Deskew, Invert, and Mirror options to correct errors that were made when the documents were scanned. These tools can be used with any image type. They use single-image optimization to speed up the editing process.

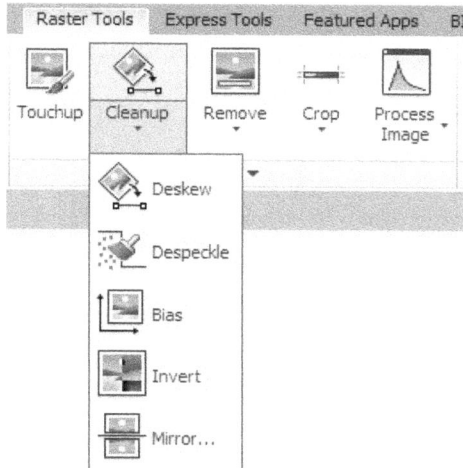

Single-Image Optimization

If you only have one image inserted in the current drawing, it is automatically selected by the single-image optimization when you run a command. You are only prompted to select an image if you are working with multiple images, which simplifies the image-editing process.

Deskew

You use the Deskew tool to rotate a raster image in its frame, usually to align it orthogonally with the AutoCAD® coordinate system. This change is saved in the image file.

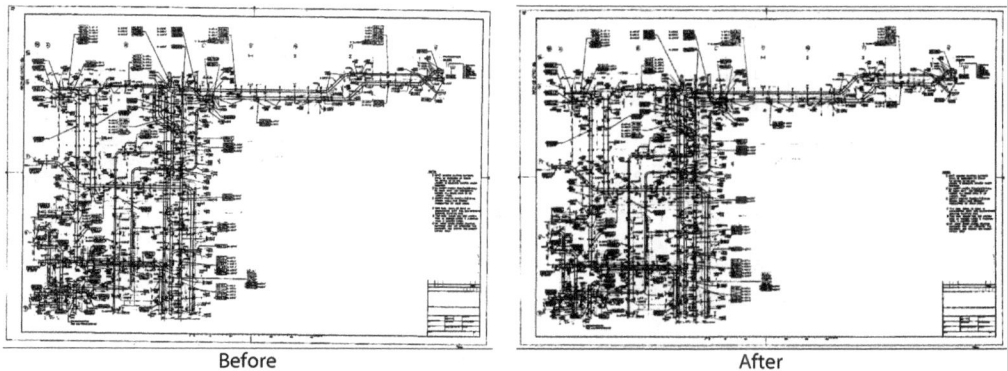

| Before | After |

Deskewing an image is similar to using the AutoCAD Rotate tool. The main difference is that the Rotate tool changes the frame of the image, and the Deskew tool changes the contents of the frame.

Example

A drawing that was placed on a flat-bed scanner at an angle looks crooked when you insert it in a drawing. Use the Deskew tool to permanently remove the angle so that the image displays correctly when it is used.

If you rotate an image using grips or the AutoCAD Rotate tool, it is not permanently changed and you need to rotate it each time you insert the image.

Inverting and Mirroring Images

Invert

Inverting an image reverses the light and dark shades of any binary, color, or grayscale image. If an image was scanned as a negative, you can invert it to create a positive image, and vice-versa.

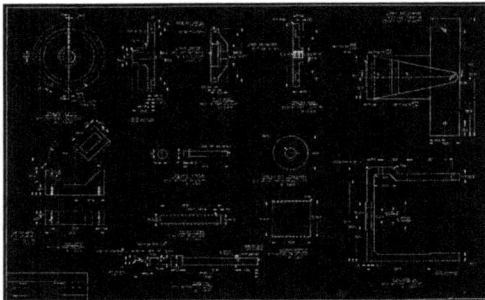
Before

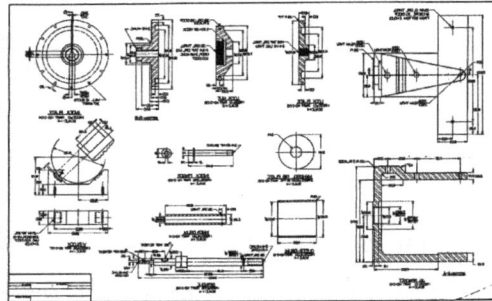
After

Mirror

When you mirror an image, you create a new version of an existing object by reflecting it in relation to a line or plane. Any image type can be mirrored.

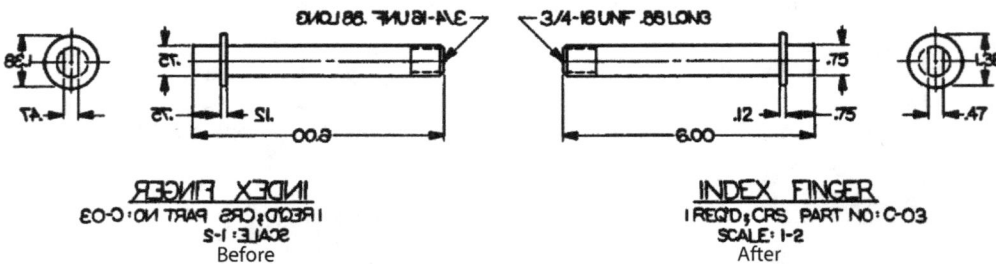
Before   After

Mirroring an image is similar to using the AutoCAD Mirror tool. However, you can only mirror an image about a horizontal or vertical axis. You cannot mirror about any arbitrary line or plane.

Example

Your drawing was scanned to display white lines on a black background. When printed, this image wastes a lot of ink and any vectors drawn on top of the image are lost on the background. Use the Invert tool to reverse the colors and have the image print as black lines on a white background.

Guidelines for Fixing Scanning Errors

Three image-editing tools are covered: Deskew, Invert, and Mirror. They are used on images immediately after they have been inserted. Most of these tools are very simple and do not require options.

The following basic guidelines for using the tools ensure the best possible results:

- Use Raster Snaps and Osnaps to select points accurately.
- These editing commands can be used with any image type.
- Because the Invert tool does not have any options, if you need to do more in-depth color editing, you can use the Palette Manager or Histogram editing tools.

Mirror Options

Unlike the Deskew and Invert tools, the Mirror tool has the following options:

Option	Description
Top to Bottom	Mirrors the image about the horizontal axis.
Side to Side	Mirrors the image about the vertical axis.

These options are available in the Mirror Options dialog box after you select the images to be mirrored.

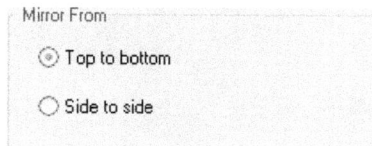

Mirror From
- ⦿ Top to bottom
- ◯ Side to side

Example

The following are common scenarios in which you might need to edit a scanned image:

- A white-line blueprint was scanned as a binary image for vectorization or raster entity manipulation. For these tasks, you need the linework to be the opposite of the AutoCAD background color. Therefore, the image might need to be inverted.
- You have scanned a photographic negative and want it to be inverted for drafting and presentation purposes.
- You are using a sheet-feed scanner and the original was fed in at an angle. You need to remove the resulting rotation.
- A mylar sheet was scanned with the wrong side up, and the image needs to be mirrored.

Scanning Images and Editing Errors

Many types of scanners and scanning software enable you to preview scans and correct any errors that might result. However, sometimes these errors might not be noticed due to a small preview window or subtle errors, such as a small amount of skew. It is recommended that you insert these images in a blank drawing and use the image cleanup tools to fix the errors.

Procedure: Fixing Errors Introduced in the Scanning Process

For the best results use the following procedure:

1. Scan the image and review the results in the scanning software. If editing tools are provided, fix any errors displayed in the preview window. This process varies depending on the scanning software used.

2. Insert the image to be edited in a new, empty drawing.

3. If there is more than one error in the image, use one of the editing tools to correct the first error.

4. Verify the results of the tool.

5. If required, use another tool to edit the next error.

If the editing process does not improve the image, you should undo the results of the command before trying another tool or retrying the original tool.

Exercise: Deskew an Image

In this exercise, you will use the Deskew tool to rotate an image in its frame.

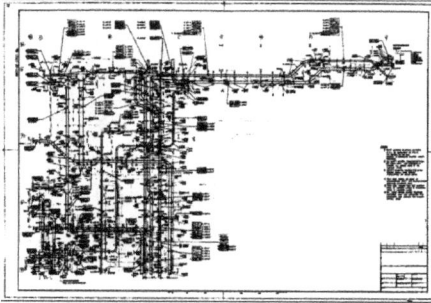

The completed exercise

1. Open ...*Fixing Errors in Scanned Drawings\ Hydro1.dwg*.

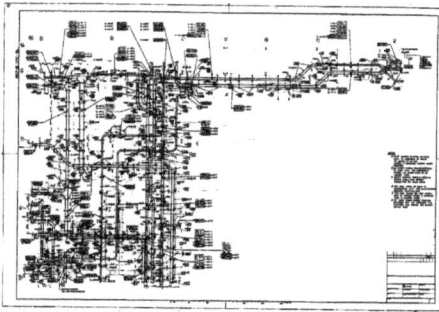

2. In the Raster Tools tab, in the Edit panel, expand the Cleanup flyout and click Deskew.

3. Deskew the image:
    - Enter **0,0** as the base point. This is the bottom-left corner of the sheet border.
    - Define the source angle by selecting the bottom-left and bottom-right corners of the border of the raster image (inside the sheet border).
    - Press ENTER to accept the default of 0 for the destination angle.

4. Zoom to the extents of the drawing and note how the image is straightened.

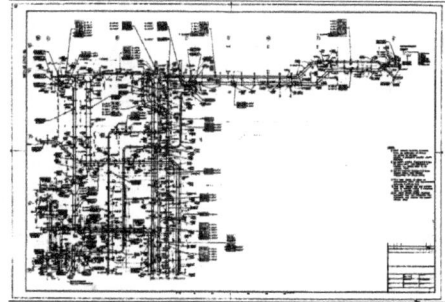

Exercise: Invert and Mirror an Image

In this exercise, you will use the Invert and Mirror tools to edit the appearance of an image.

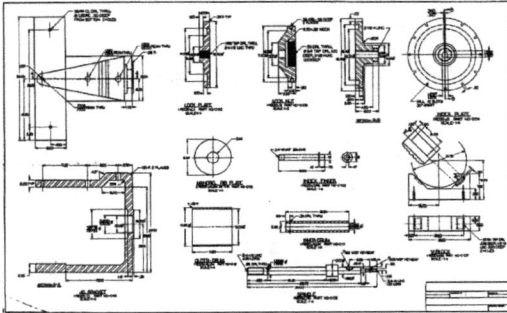

The completed exercise

5. Click OK. Note that the image displays correctly.

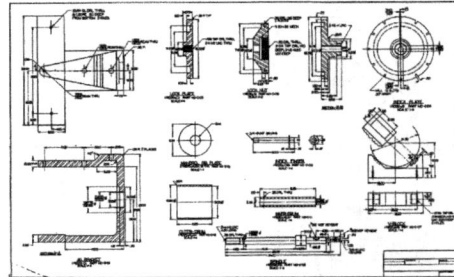

1. Open ...*Fixing Errors in Scanned Drawings\ConcDetail.dwg*. The background in the image is black.

2. In the Raster Tools tab, in the Edit panel, expand the Cleanup flyout and click Invert.

   This inverts the appearance of the image. Note that the image was scanned incorrectly and must be mirrored about the vertical axis (side to side) to be read correctly.

3. In the Raster Tools tab, in the Edit panel, expand the Cleanup flyout and click Mirror.

4. In the Mirror Options dialog box, under Mirror From, click Side to side.

Lesson: Using the Bitonal Filters

Overview

In this lesson you learn how to use a number of tools to improve the appearance of binary images, primarily to enhance the clarity of the linework in scanned black-and-white drawings.

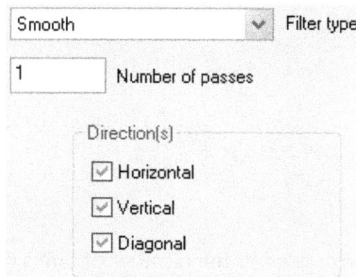

Smooth ⌄	Filter type

1	Number of passes

Direction(s)
- ☑ Horizontal
- ☑ Vertical
- ☑ Diagonal

Depending on the quality of the original document, the scanned linework might have gaps or inconsistent line widths. Improved raster lines in an image increase the clarity of its plot. In addition, working with raster entity manipulation and vectorization tools is much easier with a clearer image.

Objectives

After completing this lesson, you will be able to:

- Define the terms used in working with bitonal filters and describe the different filter types.
- Determine when bitonal filters should be used on a raster image.
- Describe how the use of bitonal filters fits into the overall raster image editing process.
- Smooth, thin, and thicken raster lines.
- Separate partially merged lines and use the Skeletonize filter.

About Bitonal Filters

The Bitonal Filters dialog box has two options and five filter types:

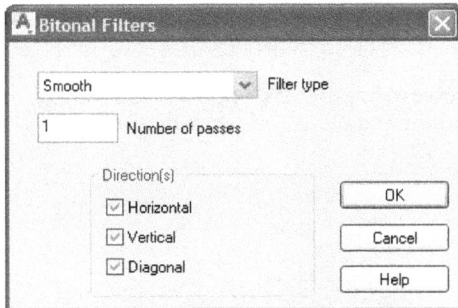

Number of Passes

The Number of Passes option in the Bitonal Filters dialog box specifies the number of times the filter runs. For example, a pass value of 3 runs the command three times.

Direction(s)

The Direction(s) option controls how pixels are added or removed from the raster linework. Horizontal, vertical, diagonal, or any combination of these directions can be selected.

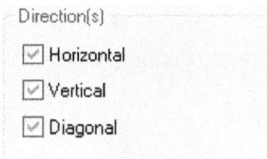

Bitonal Filter Types

There are five types of bitonal filters:

Filter	Description
Smooth	Removes unnecessary pixels from the edges of raster objects, fills holes in raster lines, and removes speckles from the raster image.
Thin	Trims raster objects by one pixel (per pass) in all directions.
Thicken	Thickens the edges of raster objects by one pixel (per pass) in the specified directions.
Separate	Separates raster lines that are partially merged to prevent being converted into one thick line.
Skeletonize	Thins all of the raster data to a thickness of one pixel. The Skeletonize filter does not use the number of passes and processing direction options.

Example

If you scan an image from a faded original, some areas might lack data or have spots or gaps in the linework. You can use the Smooth filter to improve the image for use as a background.

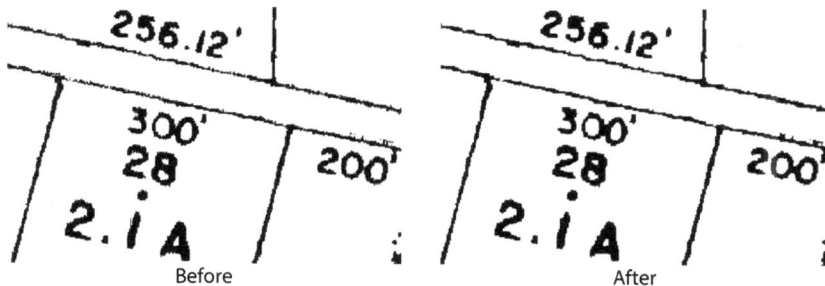

Before   After

When to Use Bitonal Filters

Bitonal filters can be used to improve the appearance of bitonal images or to simplify the linework before using vectorization tools. These filters can be used at any time when working with a black and white (bitonal) image. Generally, you should use these filters before using other raster editing tools. If you are not happy with the results of running a filter, you can use the Undo tool and try a different filter.

Bitonal Filter Guidelines

Note the following guidelines when using these filters:

- These filters only work on bitonal (black-and-white) images.
- Single-image optimization is available for the bitonal filters.
- You can only process one image at a time.
- You can process a portion of an image if the issues are confined to one area.
- You can use more than one filter on the same image. For example, you can use the Smooth filter to make the lines more consistent and use the Thin filter to reduce the width of the lines.

Example

You have a scanned floor plan that is going to be used as the basis of a remodeling project. Since the project is going to be done entirely in CAD, you need to convert the image. The scan itself is of fairly poor quality. You can use the Smooth, Thicken, and Thin filters to improve the consistency of the scan to make the vectorization more accurate.

Processing Bitonal Images

The use of a bitonal filter is one step in the overall process of editing raster images. Generally, images that require editing using Vectorization Tools or Raster Entity Manipulation require a certain amount of consistency and conformity in the image. If the linework in the raster image has problems, such as varying thickness, gaps, or overlaps, the editing tools might not produce the required results. Using bitonal filters as a step in the editing process can assist in generating a more accurate end product.

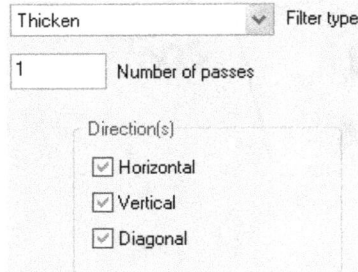

Procedure: Editing an Image Including Bitonal Filters

Use the following steps to use bitonal filters in the image editing process.

1. Insert the image into the current drawing.

2. Verify that the image is bitonal (black and white). If it is not, you can use the Change Color Depth or Histogram commands to convert the image.

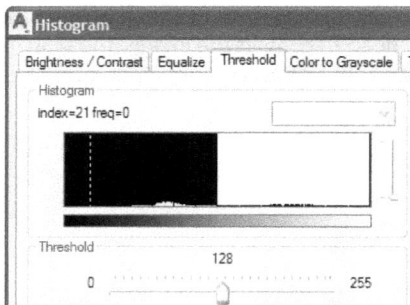

3. Use the Bitonal Filters tool to process the image. If required, run the command again to apply additional filters to the image.

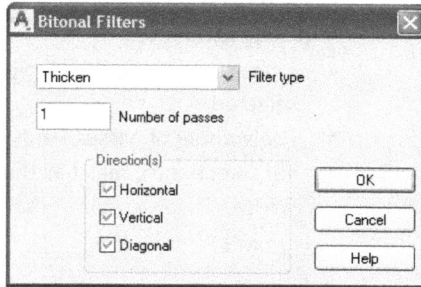

4. Once the image has been processed, you can use other options, such as the Vectorization Tools or Raster Entity Manipulation to further edit the image.

Exercise: Smooth, Thin, and Thicken Raster Lines

In this exercise, you will use several of the bitonal filters to improve the appearance of raster lines.

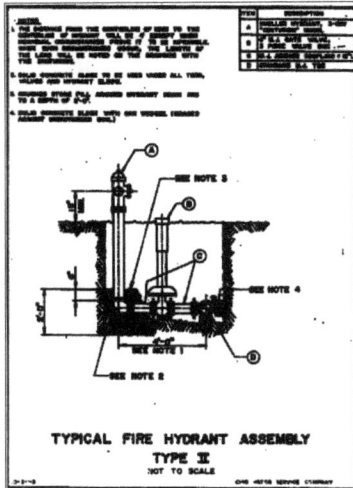

The completed exercise

1. Open ...*Using the Bitonal Filters\H1.dwg*.

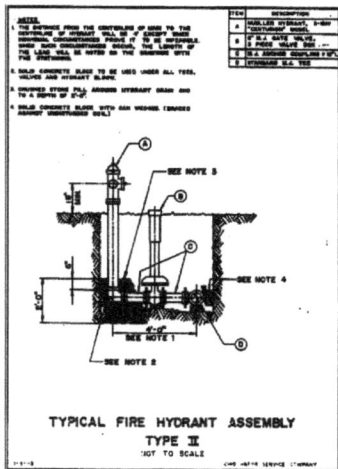

2. In the Raster Tools tab, in the Edit panel, expand the Process Image flyout and click Bitonal Filters. Press ENTER to select the entire image.

3. In the Bitonal Filters dialog box, verify the following settings:

   - For Filter type, verify that Smooth is selected.
   - For Number of passes, verify that **1** is set.
   - For Direction(s), select all three check boxes.

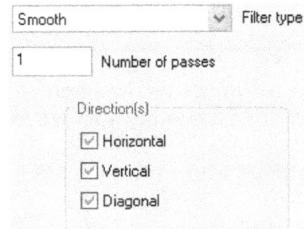

4. Click OK.

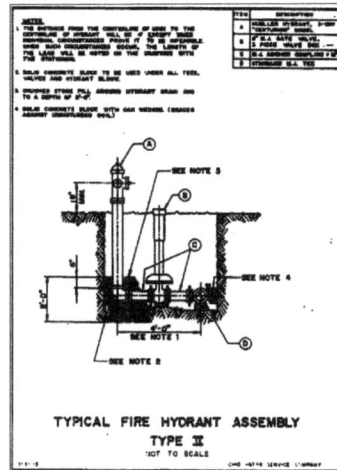

5. Click Undo to remove the smoothing filter.

6. In the Raster Tools tab, in the Edit panel, expand the Process Image flyout and click Bitonal Filters. Press ENTER to select the entire image.

7. In the Bitonal Filters dialog box, specify the following settings:
   - For Filter type, select Thin.
   - For Number of passes, enter **1**.
   - For Direction(s), select all three check boxes.

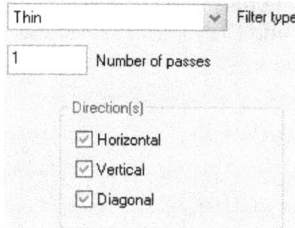

8. Click OK. Note that the content in the image is thinned.

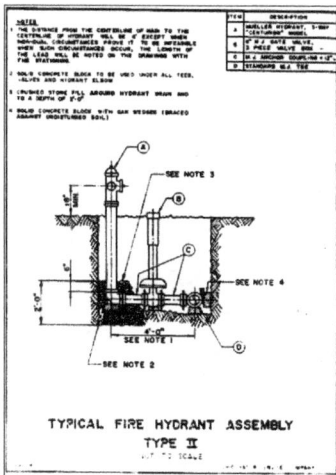

9. Click Undo to remove the thinning filter.

10. In the Raster Tools tab, in the Edit panel, expand the Process Image flyout and click Bitonal Filters. Press ENTER to select the entire image.

11. In the Bitonal Filters dialog box, specify the following settings:
    - For Filter type, select Thicken.
    - For Number of passes, enter **1**.
    - For Direction(s), select all three check boxes.

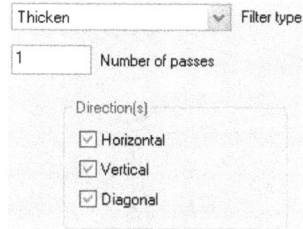

12. Click OK.

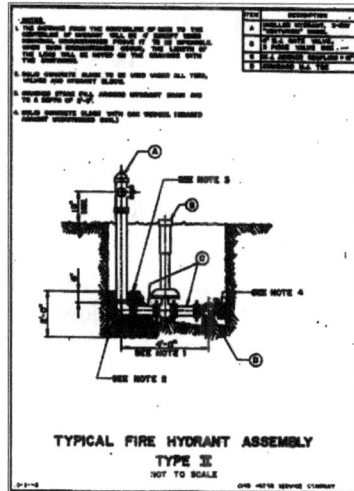

Exercise: Separate Partially Merged Lines and Use Skeletonize

In this exercise, you will edit a scanned image to separate lines that seem to merge and you will convert all of the linework to a consistent width.

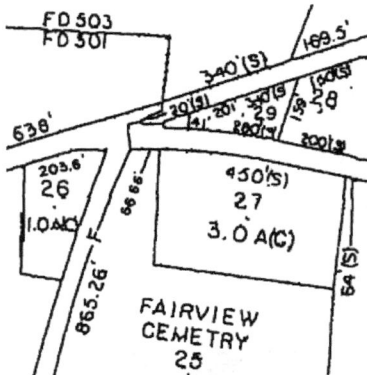

The completed exercise

1. Open ...\Using the Bitonal Filters\ TopoLines.dwg.

2. In the Raster Tools tab, in the Edit panel, expand the Process Image flyout and click Bitonal Filters.

3. Draw a window around the current display of the drawing as shown in the following illustration.

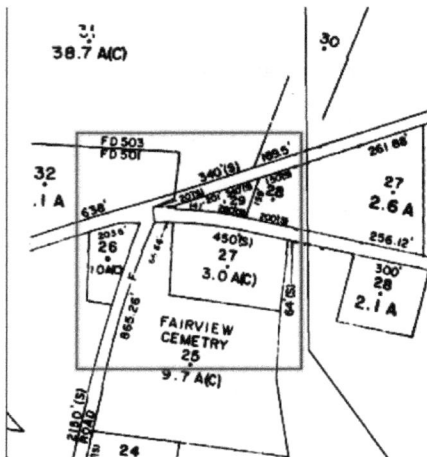

4. In the Bitonal Filters dialog box, specify the following settings:

    ▪ For Filter type, select Separate.
    ▪ For Number of passes, verify that **1** is set.
    ▪ For Direction(s), verify that Horizontal, Vertical, and Diagonal are selected.

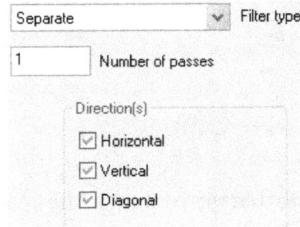

5. Click OK.

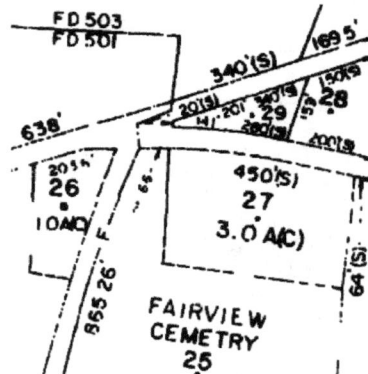

6. Click Undo to remove the Separate filter.

7. In the Raster Tools tab, in the Edit panel, expand the Process Image flyout and click Bitonal Filters. Press ENTER to select the entire image.

8. In the Bitonal Filters dialog box, for Filter Type, select Skeletonize.

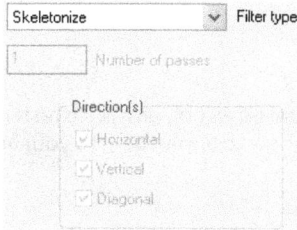

9. Click OK. Note that the image becomes dim.

10. In the Raster Tools tab, in the Edit panel, expand the Process Image flyout and click Bitonal Filters. Press ENTER to select the entire image.

11. In the Bitonal Filters dialog box, specify the following settings:

- For Filter type, select Thicken.
- For Number of passes, enter **1**.
- For Direction(s), verify that Horizontal, Vertical, and Diagonal are selected.

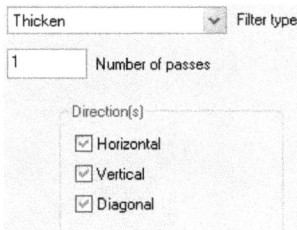

12. Click OK.

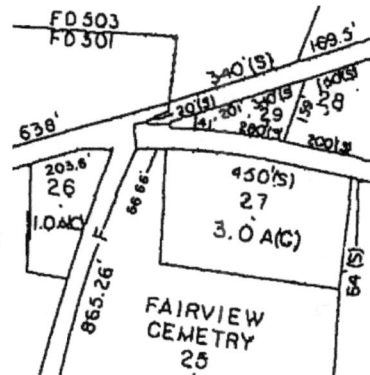

Lesson: Using the Convolve Filters

Overview

You use convolve filters to correct defects in, and enhance the visual aspect of, grayscale raster images. In this lesson you learn about the different filter types and how to apply them to your images.

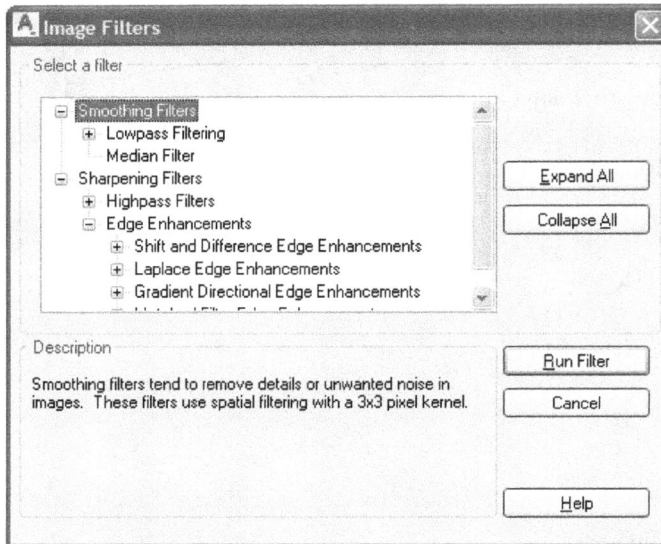

You can improve the appearance of grayscale images by using the convolve filters to remove noise or enhance contrast.

Objectives

After completing this lesson, you will be able to:

- Define the terms used when working with convolve filters.
- Determine when convolve filters should be used on a raster image.
- Describe how the use of convolve filters fits into the overall raster image editing process.
- Use a convolve filter to edit a grayscale image.

About Convolve Filters

Each of the two main categories of convolve filter types (smoothing and sharpening) has several groups of filters. The following filter types are commonly used to edit grayscale images.

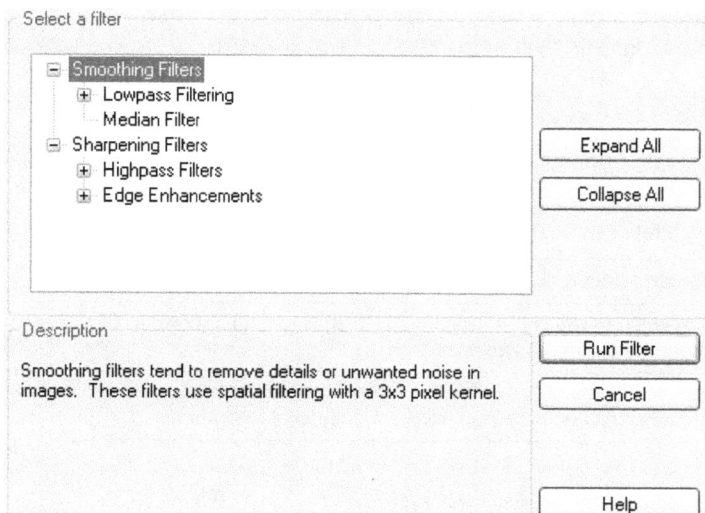

Select a filter

- Smoothing Filters
  - Lowpass Filtering
  - Median Filter
- Sharpening Filters
  - Highpass Filters
  - Edge Enhancements

Expand All

Collapse All

Description

Smoothing filters tend to remove details or unwanted noise in images. These filters use spatial filtering with a 3x3 pixel kernel.

Run Filter

Cancel

Help

Smoothing Filters

Smoothing filters reduce the harshness and visual noise in a grayscale image. You use them to remove small details from your image that are noise rather than useful data.

- Smoothing Filters
  - Lowpass Filtering
    - Lowpass Filter #1
    - Lowpass Filter #2
    - Lowpass Filter #3
    - Lowpass Filter #4
    - Blurring
  - Median Filter

Sharpening Filters

Sharpening filters make differences in shading more distinct, such as when you need highpass filters to extract the highest amount of useful data from a low-resolution scan.

- Sharpening Filters
  - Highpass Filters
  - Edge Enhancements
    - Shift and Difference Edge Enhancements
    - Laplace Edge Enhancements
    - Gradient Directional Edge Enhancements
    - Matched Filter Edge Enhancements

Smoothing Filter Types

The following groups of smoothing filters can be used:

Filter Type	Description
Lowpass	In areas where pixel intensities change rapidly, lowpass filters can lessen the severity of the change by reducing the high-frequency detail in an image. This results in a slightly blurred image.
Median	Changes each pixel value to match the average value of the neighboring pixels.

Sharpening Filter Types

The following sharpening filters can be used:

Filter Type	Description
Highpass	Can enhance the edges in an image. Images that do not display clearly can be sharpened using Highpass filtering.
Edge Enhancements	Use to easily identify boundaries and property lines. You can also use these filters for object extraction or recognition by higher-level algorithms.

Example

The series of aerial photographs that you are using for a public hearing on a new project were scanned and the results are not clear. The details of the existing buildings, roads, and bridges are not displayed clearly. You can use the Edge Enhancements sharpening filters to improve the appearance of these photographs and to enhance the details of the site features.

When to Use Convolve Filters

Convolve filters can be used to improve the appearance of grayscale images before using other editing tools or printing. Convolve filters can be used at any time when working with a grayscale image. If the results of running a filter are not as required, you can use the Undo tool and try a different filter.

Convolve Filter Guidelines

Note the following when using convolve filters:

- These filters only work with grayscale images.
- Single-image optimization is available for convolve filters.
- Convolve filters are applied to the entire image.
- Convolve filters have many options. The dialog box contains options for using each of the filters.

Example

You have an aerial photograph taken with older equipment, which has a lot of noise. You need to use this photograph as the background in a public presentation piece. You can use a smoothing filter to reduce the noise before printing.

If you need to have more finely tuned control over the brightness, contrast, or other options, use the Histogram tool.

Processing Grayscale Images

Using a convolve filter is one step in the overall process of editing raster images. Generally, grayscale images are used in the backgrounds of drawings to indicate elements, such as project areas. Although you can use other tools to adjust elements, such as brightness and contrast, these are linear editing tools and might not address certain issues, such as edge sharpness or removal of noise, as indicated by spikes in a histogram. Using convolve filters before using other raster editing tools can result in a much cleaner appearance in the final work product.

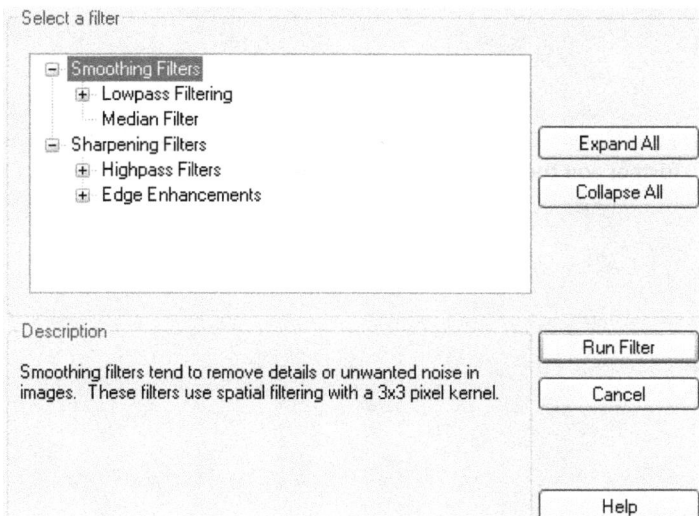

Procedure: Editing an Image Including Convolve Filters

To use convolve filters in the image editing process, use the following steps:

1. Insert the image into the current drawing.

2. Verify that the image is grayscale. If not, you can use the Change Color Depth or Histogram tools to convert the image.

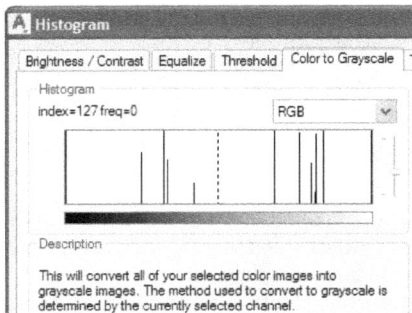

3. Use the Convolve Filters tool to process the image.

4. Once the image has been processed, you can use other options, such as the Histogram or Image Properties to further edit the properties, such as the brightness and contrast of the image.

Exercise: Use the Convolve Filters

In this exercise, you will enhance an image using the convolve filters.

The completed exercise

1. Open ...\Using the Convolve Filters\ Highrise.dwg.

2. In the Raster Tools tab, in the Edit panel, expand the Process Image flyout and click Convolve.

3. In the Image Filters dialog box, click to expand Smoothing Filters and select Median Filter.

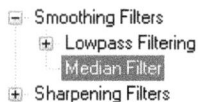

    ⊟ Smoothing Filters
        ⊞ Lowpass Filtering
            Median Filter
    ⊞ Sharpening Filters

4. Click Run Filter.

5. In the Median Filter dialog box, for Filter size, enter **5**.

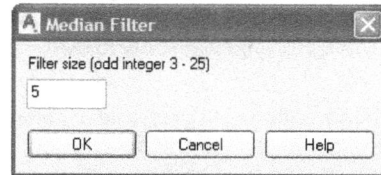

6. Click OK.

The image is filtered and most of the black noise in the buildings' shadows is removed. A higher Filter Size number would remove more of the black areas.

Lesson: Working with a Histogram

Overview

In this lesson you learn how to use histogram editing to adjust images and to change an image's color depth.

When working with grayscale or color images, what you see is not always what you get. There might be differences in brightness and contrast between the original image, the image on your computer monitor, and the final printout. Scanners, digital cameras, monitors, and printers all use different internal settings for brightness and contrast on all color channels. The AutoCAD® Raster Design software contains tools for adjusting the colors in an image and for converting images from color to grayscale or black and white. You can make all of these edits in a histogram.

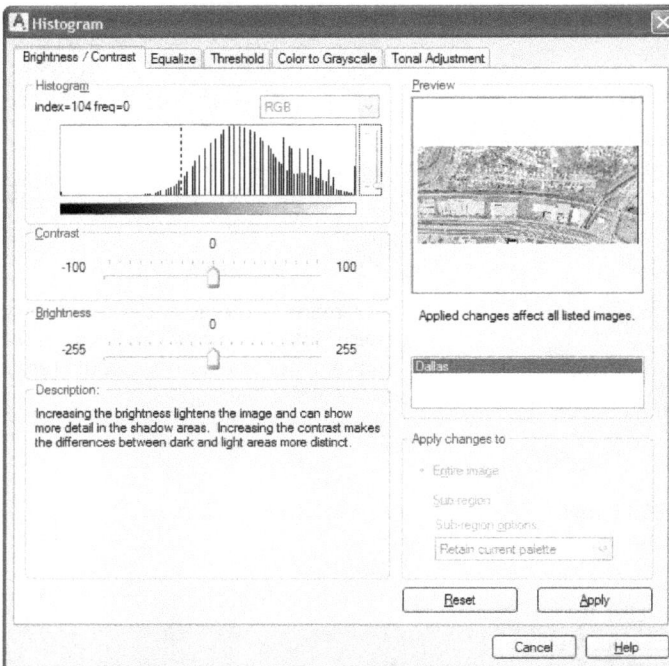

Objectives

After completing this lesson, you will be able to:

- Describe a histogram and how it works.
- Identify the different types of image adjustments that can be made.
- Define the terms used when converting images with a histogram.
- Determine when histogram editing should be used on an image.
- Use a histogram to adjust an image.
- Convert an image to binary.

About the Histogram

Pixels

The term pixel is short for picture element. Pixels are single dots that form raster images on the screen and can be individually assigned different colors or shades of gray.

Color Channels

Color images are often represented by a mix of red, green, and blue hues, similar to the way a color monitor works. For image editing, these color channels can be separated and balanced individually.

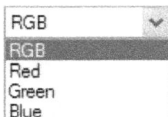

Histogram

A histogram is a graph displaying the distribution of pixels in an image across the color map. The range of shades depends on the selected image type. The darker shades are shown on the left side of the graph and the lighter shades on the right. You can use histogram editing on this distribution to change the appearance of an image. When editing a color image, you can work on the histogram for the entire image or for the individual color channels.

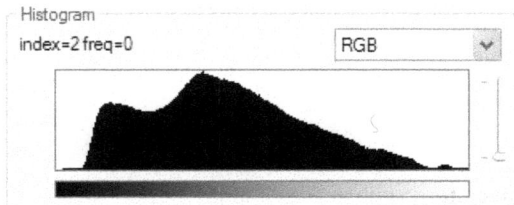

> You can only use histogram editing on grayscale and color images and not on black-and-white (bitonal) images.

Histogram Elements

The histograms used in the AutoCAD Raster Design software use the following elements.

Element	Description
Index	A number listed in the upper-left corner of the histogram that represents the color numbers used by the image.
Frequency	A number listed in the upper-left corner of the histogram that indicates the number of pixels using each shade in the image.
Shade Bar	A bar that extends across the bottom of the histogram to preview the actual shade represented by each index.

An example of a histogram using the three elements is shown in the following illustration.

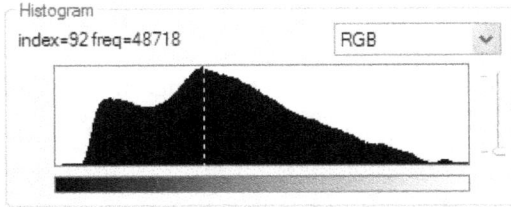

Histogram Types

The types of histograms are as follows:

Type	Description
Input Histogram	Displays in gray as a background image that provides a reference to the changes being made.
Output Histogram	Displays in black as a foreground image that displays a preview of the effect of your changes before they are applied to the actual image.

The output histogram overlaid on an input histogram is shown in the following illustration.

About Adjusting Images

You can use the three tools in the Histogram editor to enhance an image. They are located in the Brightness/Contrast, Equalize, and Tonal Adjustment tabs in the Histogram dialog box.

Brightness

Brightness is a measurement of the amount of lightness or darkness displayed by the pixel distribution. Increasing the brightness of an image shifts all of the pixels to the lighter end of the histogram, increasing the number of pixels that display as white. Decreasing the brightness of an image shifts all of the pixels to the darker end of the histogram, increasing the number of pixels that display as black.

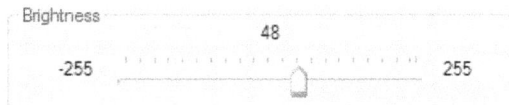

Contrast

Contrast measures the amount of variation between shades in an image. Increasing the contrast decreases the tonal gradation between the highlights, midtones, and shadows in an image. Decreasing the contrast increases the tonal gradation and results in a wider range of shades.

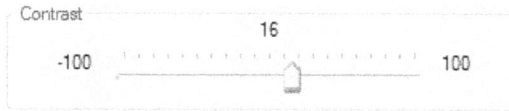

Equalize

When you equalize an image, the darkest pixels are changed to black and the lightest pixels are changed to white. The remaining pixels are then reassigned to use all of the colors in between. This is also called a nonlinear contrast stretch. Equalizing can enhance the detail in a raster image.

Tonal Adjustment

Using tonal adjustment (also called nonlinear editing), you can balance the brightness and contrast of an image using differing amounts of adjustment at different points in the histogram.

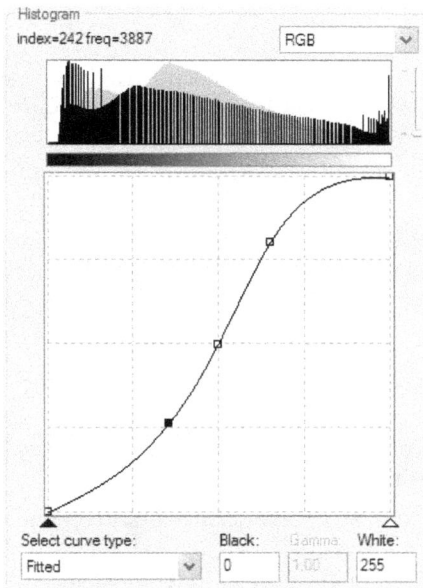

Example

You are using several digital photographs that were taken in different lighting conditions. You can more closely match the colors or shades of gray in these images using the tonal adjustment features.

This type of color matching can be difficult if you are only using a linear brightness or contrast adjustment. For better results you can vary the amount of adjustment for different portions of the histogram.

About Converting Images

In addition to enhancing images, you can change the color depth of an image using the tools in the Threshold and Color To Grayscale tabs in the Histogram dialog box.

Threshold

The Threshold tool converts a grayscale or color image to a black-and-white binary image.

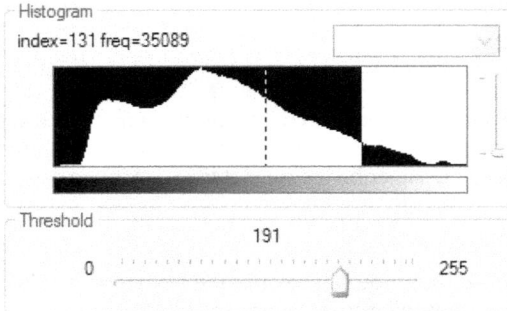

Color to Grayscale

Using the Color To Grayscale histogram tool, you can convert any color image to an 8-bit grayscale image. This is useful if you want to convert a 32- or 24-bit color image to grayscale to reduce the amount of disk space required by the image.

Example

You want to convert a color map to black-and-white to isolate specific features, such as roads or contour lines. You can use the Threshold tools to make this conversion. After saving it as a bitonal image file, you can use other tools to edit the image or convert the linework to vectors.

Guidelines for Working with Color and Grayscale Images

Although each of the histogram editing tools has its own guidelines for usage, some general guidelines for working with any of the tools include the following:

- You do not need to edit the entire image at once. You can select a portion to edit when you initially start the command.
- When working with a color image, you can use most of the histogram editing tools on any of the individual color channels. For example, you can convert just the red color channel to a grayscale image.
- Check the Preview window and note the effect of your edits before applying them to the image.
- You can use multiple tabs in the Histogram dialog box on the same image. This is useful if you want to change the brightness and contrast before altering the threshold of an image.
- Click Apply to update the image to reflect the changes.

Guidelines for Using the Histogram Editing Tools

Note the following when using the Histogram editing tools:

- Bitonal images cannot be edited using the Histogram tools.
- The image conversion tools can only be used to lower an image's color depth, not to raise it.
- Grayscale images only have one color channel.
- If you are using the Tonal Adjustment editing tools, you can export and import contrast curves between images.
- After clicking Apply, you cannot use Reset to reverse your edits.
- You can use the Undo tool to reverse the effects of histogram editing.

Exercise: Use a Histogram

In this exercise, you will learn how to read a histogram and perform simple edits by adjusting the brightness and contrast of an image.

The completed exercise

1.   Open ...\Working with a Histogram\ Dallas_AP.dwg.

2.   In the Raster Tools tab, in the Edit panel, expand the Process Image flyout and click Histogram. Press ENTER to process the entire image.

3.   In the Histogram dialog box, verify that the Brightness/Contrast tab is current.

4.   In the Histogram area, move the cursor over the histogram until the Index value displays 150.

The Frequency value (freq) displays the number of pixels in the image that use color 150, and the shade bar displays the shade associated with color 150.

5.   Under Contrast, move the slider slowly to the right to increase the contrast.

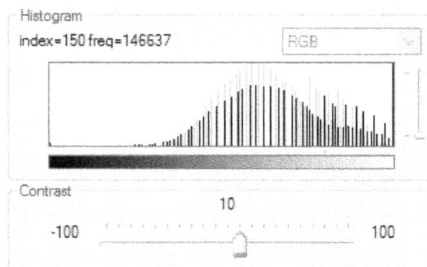

6.   Move the slider slowly to the left to decrease contrast. Note the changes in the Preview area.

7.   Click Reset to reset the contrast to 0.

8.   In the Histogram dialog box, under Brightness, move the slider to the right until it displays 125. Click Apply.

9.   Move the cursor into the histogram. All of the pixels display between color 125 and color 255.

10.   Click Close.

Exercise: Convert an Image to Binary

In this exercise, you will convert an image from color to black-and-white using the Threshold tab.

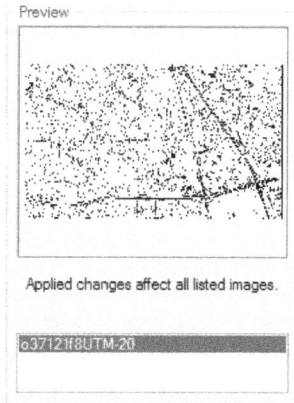

The completed exercise

1.   Open ...\Working with a Histogram\ Dublin02.dwg.

2.   In the Raster Tools tab, in the Edit panel, expand the Process Image flyout and click Histogram. Press ENTER to process the entire image.

3.   In the Histogram dialog box, click the Threshold tab.

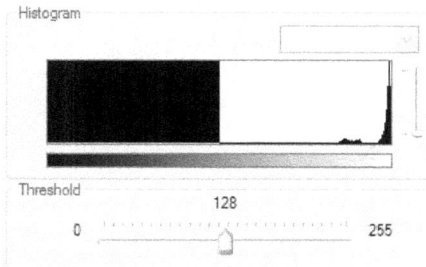

4.   Under Threshold, move the slider to the left until it displays 65.

5.   Under Threshold, move the slider to the right until it displays 190.

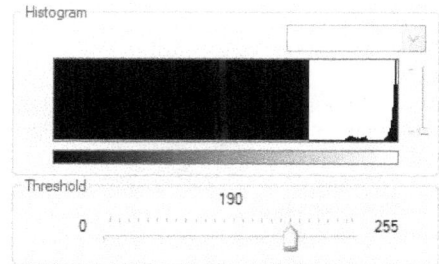

6.   In the Preview window, note how the appearance of the image has changed as a result of the thresholding.

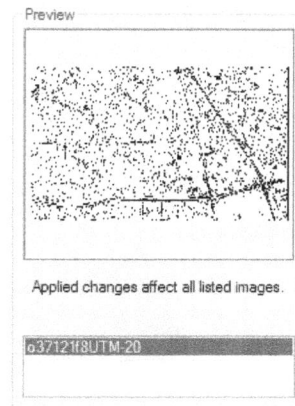

7.   Click Apply and Close.

Lesson: Controlling Colors with the Palette Manager

Overview

In this lesson you learn how to use the Palette Manager to view, modify, compress, and apply existing color palettes to grayscale or color images.

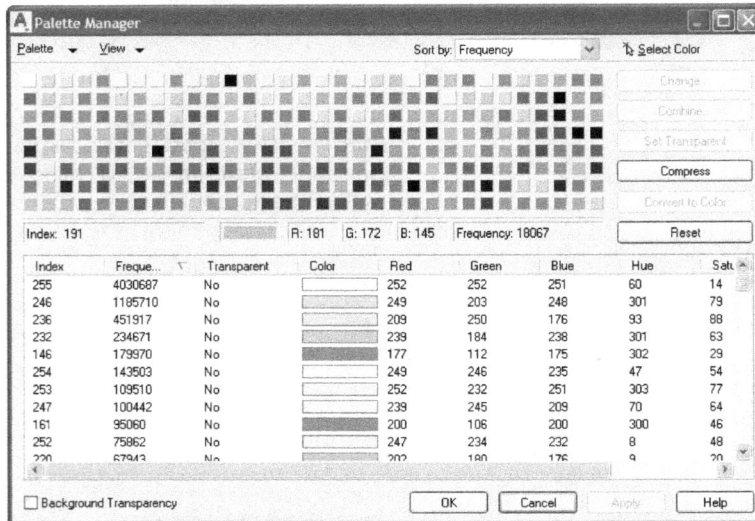

When working with an 8-bit color or grayscale image, you can use the Palette Manager to determine how the colors or shades of gray are being used.

Objectives

After completing this lesson, you will be able to:

- Define the terms used when working with color palettes.
- Define the terms used in the Palette Manager.
- Identify the types of images that can be edited using the Palette Manager.
- Prepare an image for color palette editing.
- Isolate the elements of a color image.

About Color Palettes

You can use palettes to view and edit the distribution of various shades of colors or grayscale in 8-bit images. The following terms and definitions are useful when working with these types of images.

Palette

For an 8-bit color or grayscale image, the listing of all of the shades of colors or gray in the image is referred to as a palette. The Palette Manager tools enable you to view and modify the palette of an image. Although full-color or true-color images also have palettes, they are not supported by the Palette Manager.

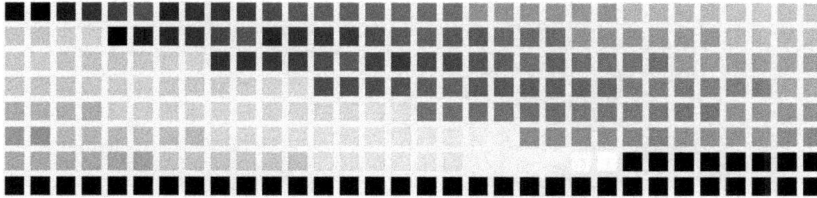

8-Bit Color Image

Also called a palette color image, an 8-bit color image supports up to 256 different shades of color. However, not all palette color images use the entire color range. When scanning images, you might select a smaller palette (such as 16 colors) for greater consistency across the image.

8-Bit Grayscale Image

Grayscale images also use up to 256 shades of gray to represent the colors in an image. As with 8-bit color images, not all shades are used. Since the shades of gray are representations of color, not all Palette Manager features are available. However, for grayscale images a button is available that can be used to convert the image to an 8-bit color image to provide access to all of the Palette Manager tools.

Web-Safe Palette

A web-safe palette reserves 40 colors for use by the computer's operating system for display in a web browser. Only 216 color indices can be used by the image.

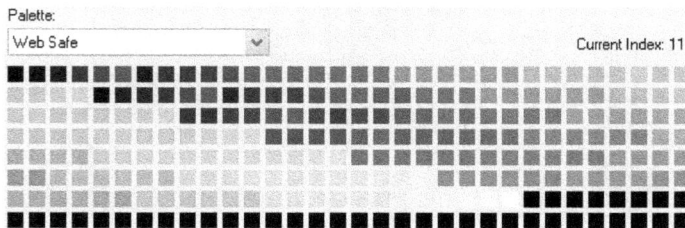

Example

You want to determine how many shades of white are used in a scanned USGS quad sheet and merge them into a single shade. You can then designate the merged shade of white as the transparent color and visually crop the border of the sheet.

You would not use the Palette Manager to change the color depth of an image to move from true color to palette color.

Terms Used in the Palette Manager

The Palette Manager enables you to edit and apply different color palettes to an image.

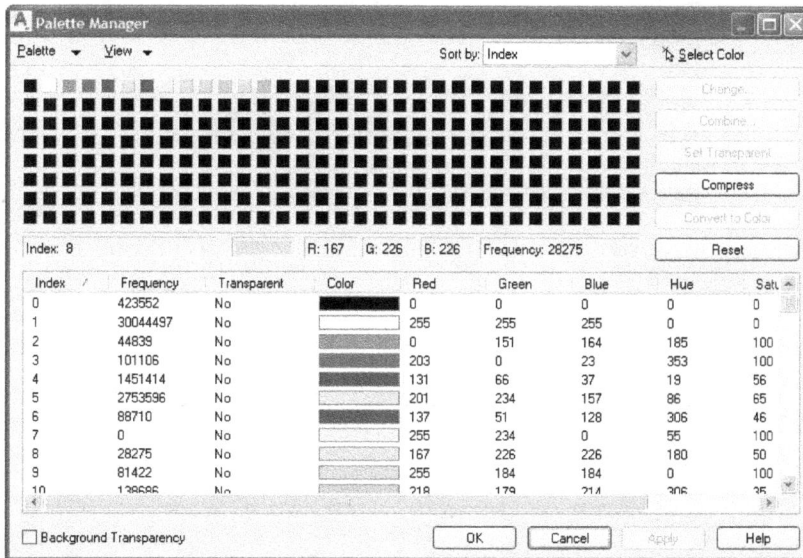

Compression

Compression removes colors that are listed in the palette, but not used in an image. This tool is primarily used after merging colors or importing a palette.

Compressing a color palette is similar to purging unused layers from the Layer Properties Manager.

Color Frequency

The number of pixels that use a specific shade is called the frequency. The higher the frequency, the more that color is used in an image. For example, if an image has a lot of white in the background, the color white has a high frequency.

Index	Frequency	Transparent	Color
0	0	No	
1	3885605	No	
2	93163	No	
3	3260	No	
4	519520	No	
5	2768590	No	
6	35	No	
7	0	No	
8	83172	No	
9	2699	No	
10	0	No	

Transparency

A transparent color is invisible for displaying and plotting purposes. You normally use transparency in areas in which you want to display underlying information, such as previously drawn vectors, or where a specific color represents a frame or background area for the image. Only one color can be transparent at a time. Setting a color to be transparent is similar to toggling off a layer.

Color Index

The color index indicates where a specific shade is located in the palette. It is similar to a color number. The index does not relate to the shade of the color or its frequency.

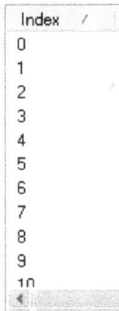

Example

You are working with an image that was originally generated in a GIS software. These often use 16 or fewer colors. If you compress the palette to remove the colors that you are not using, it is much easier to edit the remaining colors, because you do not need to scroll through the unused indices.

Palette Management Guidelines

You might need to know exactly how different colors are used in an image. The Palette Manager enables you to determine the number of colors an image uses, change an existing color to map to a different color, combine several colors into a single mapped color, compress the palette, and import or export the entire palette.

Note the following when working with palettes:

- You can only edit the color palette for one image at a time.
- If you want to use the same color palette for different images, you can export it to a palette file for future use.

Example

Using the Palette Manager provides the best results when you need to do the following:

- Identify the exact number and shades of colors in an image.
- Edit specific colors or add color to a grayscale image to emphasize the project area for presentation purposes.
- Remove or subdue features in an image by changing the color in those areas.
- Isolate features in an image, such as contour lines or watershed areas.
- Combine colors and compress the palette to reduce the number of colors used in an image to improve readability.
- Import a standard color palette, such as a web-safe palette.
- Import and export palettes between images to ensure consistency for printing purposes.
- Select a different transparency color.

Working with Color and Grayscale Images

Although the AutoCAD Raster Design software can work with 24-bit full-color images, the Palette Manager is specifically designed to work on 8-bit color or grayscale images.

Use the following guidelines when working with palettes:

- If you are working with a 24-bit color image (also called a true-color image), you can convert it to an 8-bit image using the Change Color Depth tool.
- If you are working with a grayscale image (such as a black-and-white photograph), you can use the tools in the Palette Manager to treat the shades of gray as palette colors.

Exercise: Isolate Elements of a Color Image

In this exercise, you will highlight a feature of a color image by isolating a single color, changing all other colors to a neutral background, and setting the background color to be transparent.

The completed exercise

1. Open ...\Controlling Colors with the Palette Manager\Color USGS.dwg.

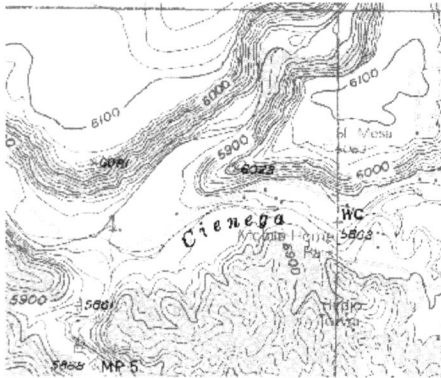

2. In the Raster Tools tab, in the Edit panel, expand the Process Image flyout and click Palette Manager.

3. Click color index 4. Right-click on the selected color and click Invert Selection.

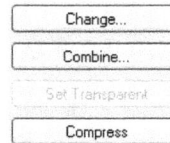

Index	Frequency	Transparent	Color	Red	Green
0	423552	No		0	0
1	30044497	No		255	255
2	44839	No		0	151
3	101106	No		203	0
4	1451414	No			
5	2753596	No		Change...	
6	88710	No		Combine...	
7	0	No		Set Background Transparency	
8	28275	No		Clear Selection	
9	81422	No		Invert Selection	
10	138896	No			

4. Click Change.

5. In the Target Color dialog box, select color index 0 (first color). Click OK.

Palette:

Current

6. Click Compress.

7. In the Palette Manage, click color index 0. Click Set Transparent.

8. Click OK. Note the color Index 4 as the isolated color.

Chapter Summary

Having completed this chapter, you can:

- Fix errors in scanned images.
- Use the bitonal filters.
- Use the convolve filters.
- Work with a histogram.
- Control colors using the Palette Manager.

Editing Images

This chapter introduces tools for editing images, including removing portions of images or directly editing raster data by copying, moving, or rotating elements of an image. These tools are helpful because scanned documents are often used as the basis for renovation or redesign projects.

Objectives

After completing this chapter, you will be able to:

- Clean up an image.
- Edit images using Raster Entity Manipulation.
- Merge vectors into raster images.

Lesson: Cleaning Up an Image

Overview

When you work on scanned documents, you can remove any portions of an image that do not need to be saved. In this lesson you learn how to use two types of tools with bitonal images: Despeckle and Remove.

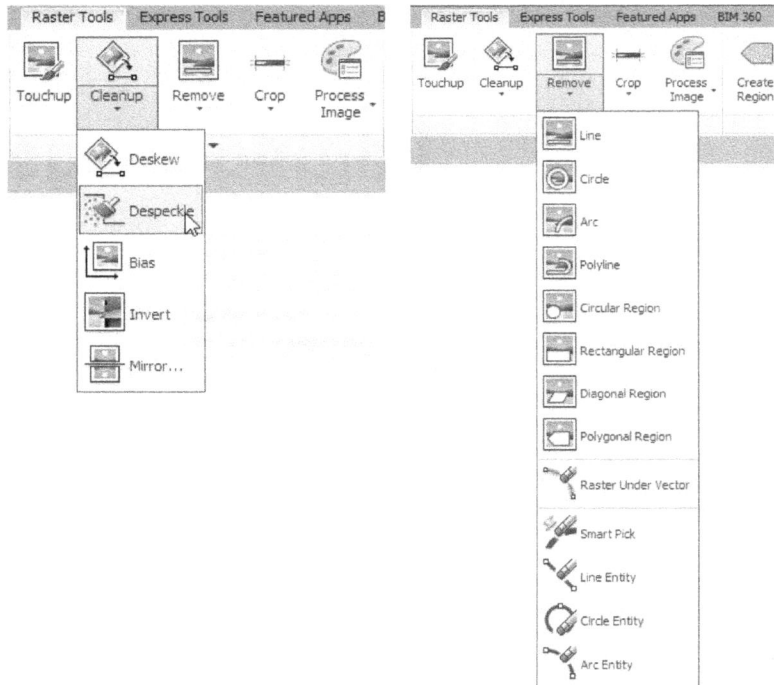

Using these tools, you can correct problems in an image, including stray pixels (a "dirty" blueprint) and faulty linework, such as bleed-throughs or incorrect as-builts.

Objectives

After completing this lesson, you will be able to:

- Define the terms used when cleaning up an image.
- Describe the options that control the behavior of the Remove tools.
- Decide when the image cleanup tools can be used.
- Explain the process of scanning images and editing when required.
- Despeckle an image.
- Remove a line using two points.
- Remove a circular region.

About Image Cleanup

To edit an image effectively, you might need to clean it up by removing defects, such as stray pixels, erroneous lines, or regions of unwanted raster data.

Despeckle

You use the Despeckle tool to remove stray pixels (speckles) from a bitonal raster image. Speckles in an image are created when you scan drawings or blueprints that are dirty or wrinkled, or when the scanner itself is dirty.

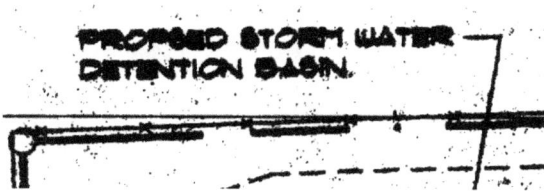

Remove

Using the Remove process (also called rub), you can delete portions of any image type. You can remove linework, such as lines, arcs, and circles, and larger portions of an image.

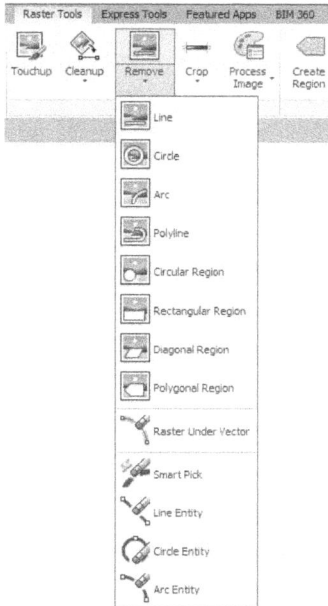

Removing portions of an image is similar to erasing elements in a vector drawing.

Example

You want to reuse a scanned detail sheet but one of the details does not apply to the new project. You can remove a polygonal area around the unneeded detail to erase it from the image.

Cleanup Options

Setting Options for the Remove Tools

Before you use the Remove tools, check the Rub / Crop Line Width setting in the AutoCAD® Raster Design Options dialog box. This option controls the size of the portion of the raster image that is affected when the Remove tools are used. The larger the value, the more raster data is removed.

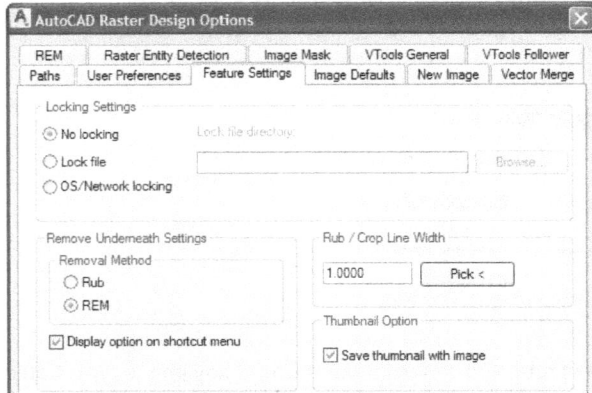

Example

You need to remove a single line from a scanned blueprint and do not want to affect any adjacent linework. By setting the Rub / Crop Line Width to a small value, you can make very fine adjustments to the image.

Image Cleanup Guidelines

Although the Despeckle and Remove tools have fairly simple results, note the following guidelines when using these tools.

Working with the Despeckle Tool

- Only works with bitonal images.
- You can only despeckle one image at a time.
- The Despeckle tool can use single-image optimization.
- You can process the portion of the image that contains the problem.
- You can deselect speckles that should not be removed, such as punctuation, decimal points, and portions of letters (such as the dot on the letter "i").

Working with the Remove Tools

- You can use the Remove tools with any image type.
- Remove tools changes the pixels in a selected area to the current transparency color. For example, if the transparency color is blue, the removed area is drawn in blue. If you subsequently change the transparency color, the color of the removed area remains blue. However, any newly removed areas are drawn in the new color.
- When you toggle on transparency for the image, the removed area becomes transparent.
- You can rub raster data in a single image or across multiple images. The only images that are affected are those that are in, or partly in, the selected entity or area.
- Use the Undo tool to reverse the effects of these commands.

Cleaning Up Scanned Images

Although many types of scanners and scanning software enable you to edit a scanned image, the types of edits that can be performed are limited. To remove areas from a scan, you can crop the image, but you generally cannot remove areas or pixels from the image. Using the Despeckle and Remove tools, you can clean up any area of the scanned image. This section describes the process of cleaning up a scanned image.

Procedure: Cleaning Up a Scanned Image

For the best results use the following steps:

1. Scan the image and review the results in the scanning software. If editing tools are provided, fix any gross errors listed in the preview window. This procedure varies depending on the scanning software used.

2. Fix any remaining major errors using the image cleanup tools, such as Deskew, Invert, and Mirror.

3. Verify that the image is bitonal. If not, convert it using the Color Depth or Histogram tools.

4. If you are using the Remove tools to modify large areas of the scanned image, verify the Rub / Crop Line Width setting in the AutoCAD Raster Design Options dialog box.

5. Use the Despeckle tool to remove stray pixels throughout the image, or the Remove tools to edit portions of the image.

If the editing process does not improve the image, you should undo the results of the command before trying another command or retrying the original command.

Exercise: Despeckle an Image

In this exercise, you will use the Despeckle tool to remove erroneous pixels or speckles from an image.

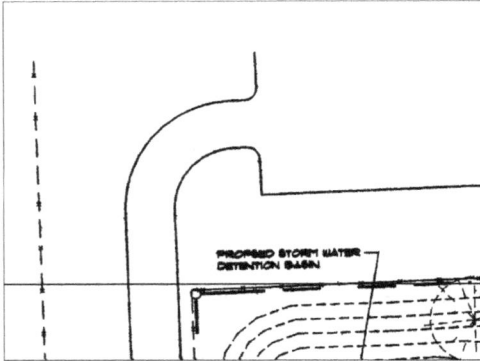

The completed exercise

1. Open ...\Cleaning Up an Image\ Landscape.dwg.

   If a Proxy Information dialog box opens, click OK.

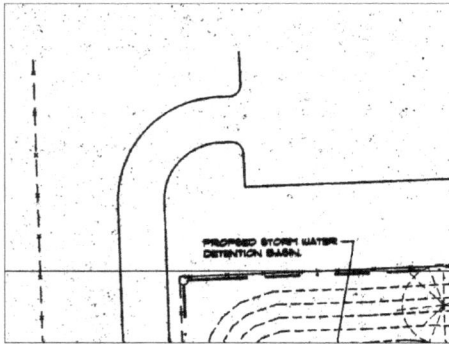

2. In the Raster Tools tab, in the Edit panel, expand the Cleanup flyout and click Despeckle.

3. Press ENTER to select the entire image. Enter **U** to enter the speckle size in AutoCAD® units. Enter **0.2** as the Speckle size in AutoCAD units.

4. Press ENTER to remove the speckles. Press ESC to exit the command.

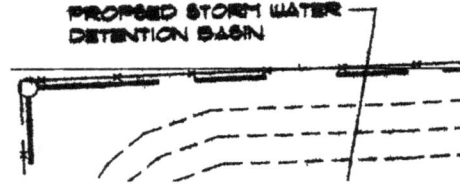

Many of the speckles are removed and the integrity of the raster lines is maintained.

Exercise: Remove a Line Using Two Points

In this exercise you will remove a raster line by selecting two points on the line. The raster between the two points will be rubbed when you change the pixels to the transparency color.

The completed exercise

1. Open ...\Cleaning Up an Image\ Cabin_01.dwg.

   If a Proxy Information dialog box opens, click OK.

   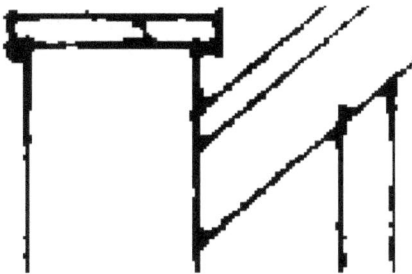

2. In the Raster Tools tab, in the Snap panel, verify that Raster Snap is not selected.

   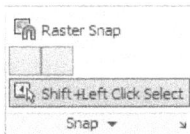

3. In the Raster Tools tab, in any panel except the Snap panel, click the Option arrow in the lower right corner to open the AutoCAD Raster Design Options dialog box.

4. Click the Feature Settings tab.

5. Set the line width:
   - Under Rub / Crop Line Width, click Pick<.
   - Pick a point directly above the lower horizontal raster line.
   - Pick the second point directly below the same line.

   It is important to manually select the line width because the Rub tool depends on the image scale.

6. Under Rub / Crop Line Width, verify the distance used. Your distance might be different.

   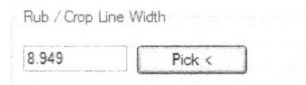

7. Click OK.

8. In the Raster Tools tab, in the Edit panel, expand the Remove flyout and click Line.

9. Specify the first point as the left end of the lower horizontal line. Specify the second point as the right end of the same line.

10. The portion of the line between the two specified points is removed.

Exercise: Remove a Circular Region

In this exercise you will remove an entire region of the raster image using several different shapes. The raster inside the area will be rubbed when you change the pixels to the transparency color.

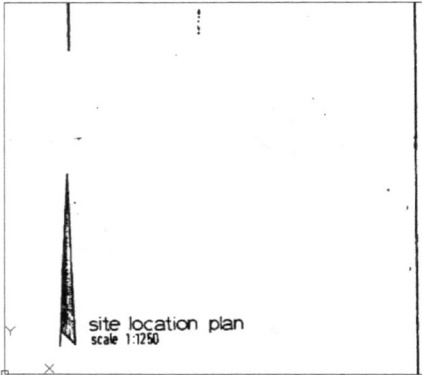

The completed exercise

1. Open ...\Cleaning Up an Image\ Cabin_05.dwg.

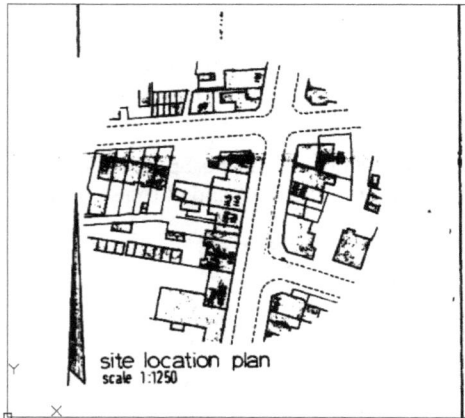

2. In the Raster tools tab, in the Edit panel, expand the Remove flyout and click Circular Region.

3. Specify the region:

- Enter **3p** to use a 3-point circle.
- Select three points that surround the circular portion of the site plan.

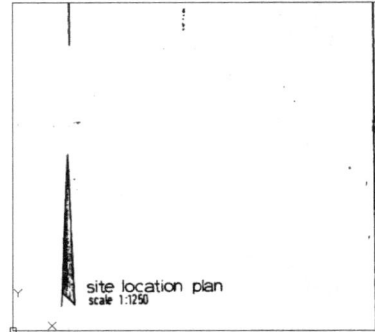

The raster data in the circular region is removed from the image.

Lesson: Editing Images Using Raster Entity Manipulation

Overview

In this lesson you learn how to select and edit portions of an image using the Raster Entity Manipulation (REM) editing tools. When you insert an image into a drawing and adjust it, you might need to edit it to remove portions of the image, or move, copy, or rotate image elements. Most image editing tools affect the entire image. However, with REM tools you can select the portion that you want to change.

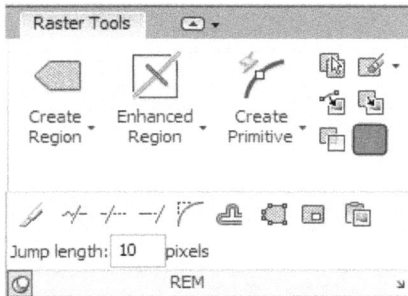

Objectives

After completing this lesson, you will be able to:

- Describe raster entity manipulation.
- Identify different types of REM selection methods.
- Determine which REM selection methods work with different types of images.
- Determine when to edit an image using raster entity manipulation.
- Edit an image using REM.

About Raster Entity Manipulation

When you use REM, you must select a portion of the image before you can make any edits.

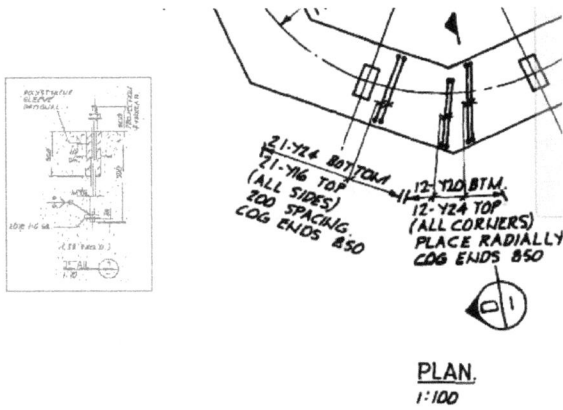

Raster Entity Manipulation Defined

You can edit portions of a raster image using REM tools to define raster entities as REM objects. After defining the REM objects, you can edit them using standard AutoCAD editing tools, such as Move and Rotate, and merge the modified raster data into the existing image or create a new image from the data.

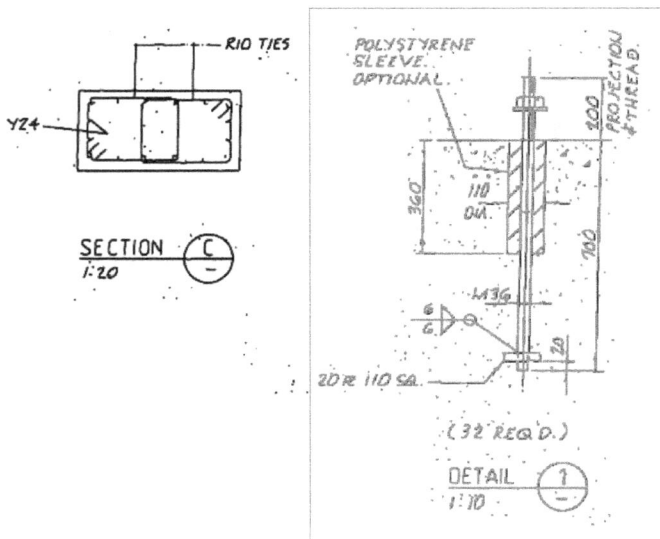

A REM object is very similar to a vector entity. The REM object has properties, such as length, radius, and scale. As with a vector entity, any of these properties can be edited.

Regions

A region is a selected area of a raster image. When working with any type of image, you can use a region object to select all of the pixels in the specified geometry, whether or not the individual raster entities consist of pixels. You can define a rectangular, polygonal, diagonal, or circular region.

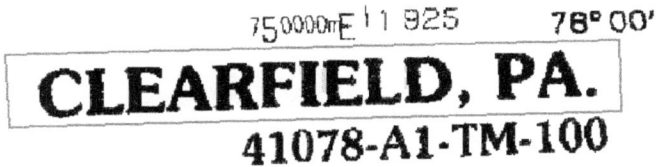

Defining a REM region is similar to cropping an image: All of the pixels in that area are selected and treated as a smaller separate image.

Example

You want to use one of the details from a detail sheet in another project. You can scan the original detail sheet, use a region to create a REM object of the required detail, and copy it to your new drawing. After pasting it, you can save the REM object as a separate raster image and use additional REM objects and editing tools to make any required changes.

You would not use REM to convert the original detail into a vector drawing. REM editing changes existing raster information, preserving the file format.

Raster Entity Manipulation and Bitonal Images

A raster entity is a series of contiguous pixels in a bitonal image that forms a single entity (such as a line, arc, or circle). Raster entities can be created as regions, enhanced bitonal regions, and primitives.

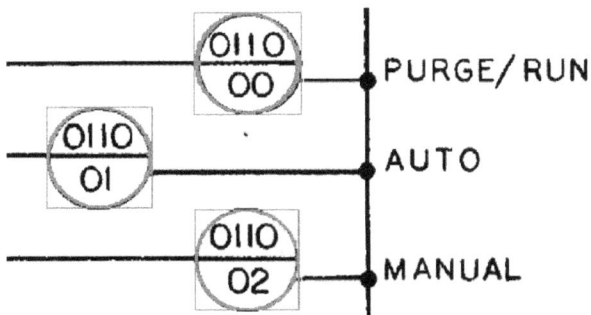

Raster entities are the image equivalents of vector entities in a drawing file.

Enhanced Bitonal Region

An enhanced bitonal region is used to select an area that contains several complete raster entities.

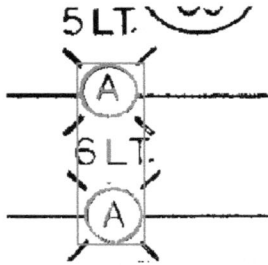

Raster entities in these regions can be selected using selection methods similar to AutoCAD window and crossing selections.

Primitives

A primitive is a selected object that is composed of a single raster entity. The three types of primitives are lines, arcs, and circles.

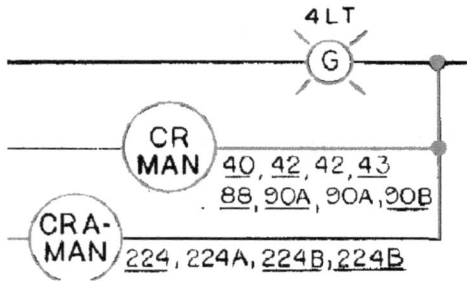

REM primitives work like their corresponding vector equivalents. These REM objects are the easiest to use when changing the actual geometry of a scanned drawing.

Smart Selection

Smart selection methods only work on bitonal images to select raster entities for defining enhanced bitonal regions or primitives. The three types of Smart selection methods are: connected areas, Smart areas, and Smart pick. Smart selection methods automatically detect the geometry of the selected raster entities and define the raster information as REM entities, such as primitive lines, arcs, or circles.

Example

You have a detail of a mechanical part that must have one of its sides extended. You scan the original detail sheet as a bitonal image and create raster entities of the side that you are going to change. You can edit these entities and merge the changes with the raster image.

You no longer need to convert the entire scanned detail to vectors to make a minor change. The scanned file can be edited directly and saved with the changes.

Raster Entity Manipulation and Image Types

Although there are many options for creating REM objects, not all of the selection methods work with all of the image types. The three types of REM selection methods and their restrictions on image types are as follows.

Method	Restrictions
Region	Can be created for any image type and resolution, including bitonal, grayscale, palette color, and true color.
Enhanced Bitonal Region	Can only be created in bitonal images.
Primitive	Can only be created in bitonal images. Can be sensitive to the zoom level of the image.

Tips for Creating REM Objects

Because REM selection methods require specific image types, and some methods have restrictions, you need to be able to convert your image.

The following techniques can help you to successfully select REM objects:

Situation	Action
You are working with a scanned drawing, (such as a floor plan or parcel map), that was scanned in color or grayscale. It must be bitonal for you to work with the individual raster entities.	In the Raster Tools tab, in the Edit panel, expand the Process Image flyout and click Change Color Depth. Enter **B** to use the Bitonal option.
You are working with an image, (such as a USGS quad sheet or aerial photograph), and it must be bitonal for you to work with raster entities rather than regions.	In the Raster Tools tab, in the Edit panel, expand the Process Image flyout and click Histogram. Click the Threshold tab. Drag the Threshold slider while watching the preview area until the appropriate raster entities display. Click Apply and Close.
You are trying to create REM primitives and the raster entity is not selected correctly.	Some REM primitive tools are sensitive to the zoom level. Zoom in or out on the image and try the tools again.

Example

You are working on a renovation project and have a blueprint that you want to edit, but it was scanned as a color image rather than bitonal. You can use the Threshold tab in the Histogram dialog box to convert it so that you can use REM primitives to change the existing layout.

When to Use Raster Entity Manipulation

You can use REM selection and editing to make minor changes in an image or when you want to enhance portions of an image. These tools are not meant to perform edits across an entire image or to convert the image to vectors.

Types of REM Editing

You can edit a REM object in many ways, including using the following options:

- AutoCAD editing tools, such as Move, Scale, Copy, and Rotate.
- Grip editing.
- Editing options in the Object Properties window.

Additionally, you can create a REM object and then create a separate image file from that object.

When to Use REM Editing

In the following scenarios, the REM editing is appropriate when:

- You need to edit a portion of an image, not the entire image.
- You want to draw attention to one portion of an image, such as an inset, or add color to a portion of a grayscale image.
- Some geometry in a scanned drawing needs to change.
- You want to copy portions of one image to another image or drawing.
- Elements of an image need to be removed while preserving intersecting or overlapping geometry.

Example

Using a REM object to create an inset, you can expand the detail of an area in an image. When you have created the REM object, resize it and save it as a separate image file.

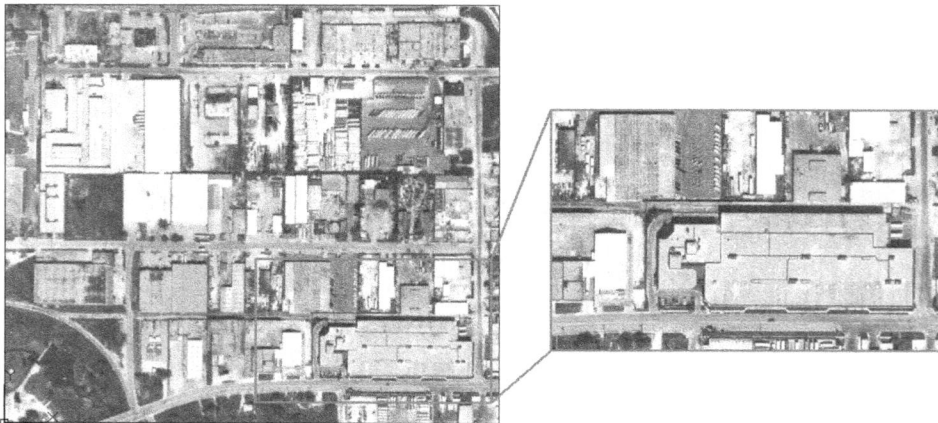

Procedure for Editing an Image Using REM

The three basic steps of editing an image with REM objects are: creating the objects, editing them, and merging them back into the image. The method of merging REM objects into the image depends on the type of editing you are performing.

Procedure: REM Image-Editing

Use the following procedure to edit an image:

1. Insert the image to be edited.
2. Verify that the image has the correct color depth for the type of REM object being used.
3. Create the REM object(s) using any of the selection methods.
4. Edit the REM objects.
5. Merge the REM objects back to the parent image.

Merging REM Objects with Parent Images

Some situations require you to remove a REM object using one of several different removal methods:

Situation	Steps
You changed the REM objects (such as by moving them), and want to merge the changes with the original image.	Select and right-click on the REM object(s). In the shortcut menu, click Merge to Raster Image.
You copied REM objects, (either to new locations in the original image or to a new image), and you want to merge the new copies and clear the original REM objects.	Select and right-click on the new REM object(s). In the shortcut menu, click Merge to Raster Image. In the Raster Tools tab, in the REM panel, click Select All and then click Clear Selected.
You created a REM object that is not correct and you want to clear it.	Select the REM object. In the Raster Tools tab, in the REM panel, click Clear Selected.
You created a REM object that you want to use as its own image, such as an inset.	Select and right-click on the REM object. In the shortcut menu, click Convert to Raster Image.

Exercise: Create and Merge a Raster Primitive

In this exercise you will use raster primitives with bitonal images. You will create an REM primitive and merge three raster images.

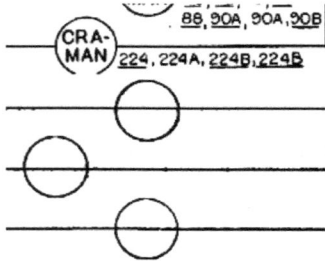

The completed exercise

1. Open ...\Editing Images Using Raster Entity Manipulation\sampling.dwg.

2. Zoom in to the upper right corner of the drawing.

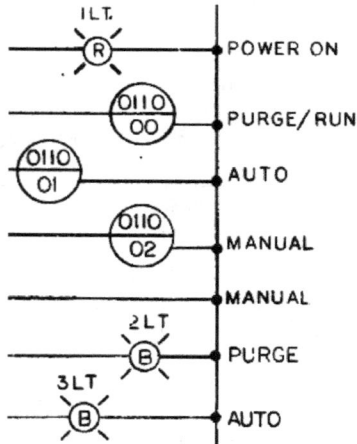

3. In the Raster Tools tab, in the REM panel, expand the Create Primitive flyout and click Circle.

4. Select a point on the large circle at the top. The circle is now a raster entity and displays in red.

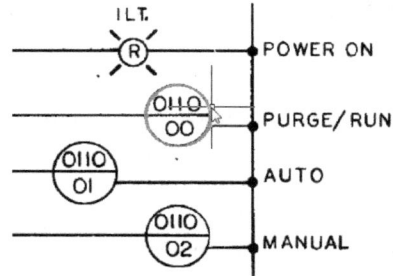

5. Right-click and click Repeat ISCIRCLE in the shortcut menu. Select another circle below it.

6. Repeat the process with the third large circle.

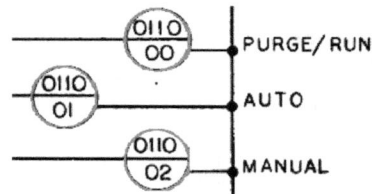

7. Zoom to the extents of the image.

8. Copy the REM circles:
    - In the Home tab, in the Modify panel, click Copy. Draw a window that fully surrounds the three raster circles. Press ENTER.
    - Enter **CEN** and press ENTER to specify the base point as the center, and then pick the top circle to specify the entity that you are using for the center.
    - Toggle Dynamic Input off, if it is on. Enter **8,15.3** to specify the second point of displacement. Press ENTER.

9. Press ENTER to end the command.

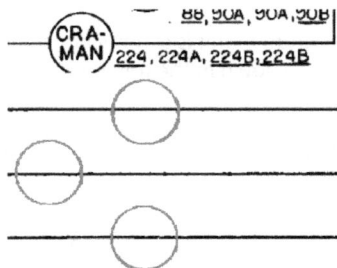

10. In the Raster Tools tab, in the REM panel, click Merge to Raster Image. Select the three raster circles that you just copied. Press ENTER.

NOTE: You might see a warning dialog box indicating that the images have copies. Click Yes to proceed.

11. In the Raster Tools tab, in the REM panel, click Select All.

12. In the Raster Tools tab, in the REM panel, click Clear Selected.

Exercise: Create an Enhanced Bitonal Region

Using a Smart Window to define an enhanced bitonal region enables you to select anything that is entirely inside the window without selecting the raster entities that are touching or crossed by the boundary of the window. In this exercise, you will create an REM enhanced bitonal region.

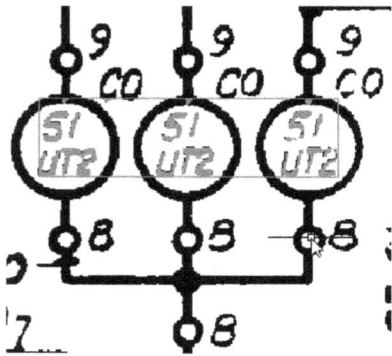

The completed exercise

1. Open ...\Editing Images Using Raster Entity Manipulation\Elec.dwg.

2. Zoom to the area of interest

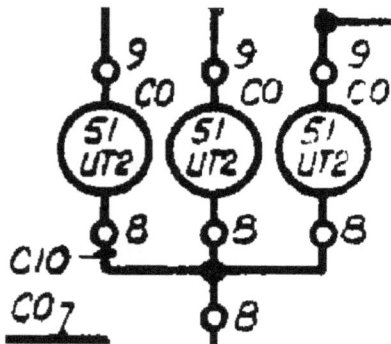

3. In the Raster Tools tab, in the REM panel, expand the Enhanced Region flyout and click Smart Window.

4. Create a window that is slightly larger than the window shown in the following illustration.

    NOTE: You might want to temporarily toggle off Raster Snaps.

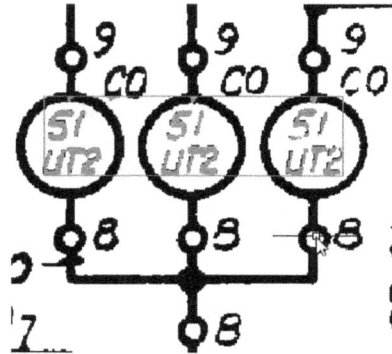

Only the text inside the circles was selected. The circles intersected the selection set but were not entirely inside the selection boundary and were not included.

5. Select and right-click on the frame of the REM region. Click Erase.

Exercise: Move, Rotate, and Merge a REM Region

In this exercise, you will move, rotate, and merge a REM region into a raster image.

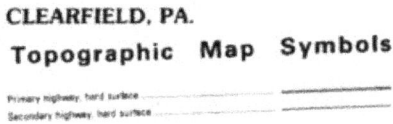

CLEARFIELD, PA.

Topographic Map Symbols

Primary highway, hard surface ....
Secondary highway, hard surface ....

The completed exercise

1. Open ...\Editing Images Using Raster Entity Manipulation\Clearfld 03.dwg.

2. Zoom to the lower right corner of the drawing.

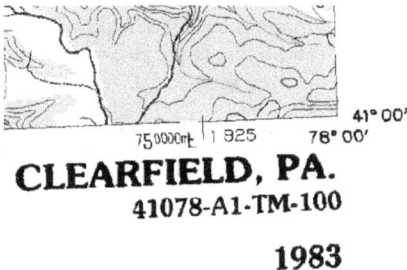

3. In the Raster Tools tab, in the REM panel, expand Create Region, and click Diagonal.

4. Click the two left corners and then select a third corner on the right side to create a diagonal window as shown in the following illustration.

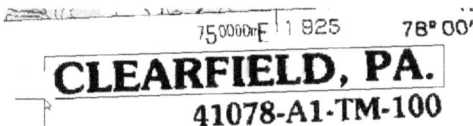

A REM region is created around the words CLEARFIELD, PA.

5. Zoom to the extents of the image.

6. In the Home tab, in the Modify panel, click Move.

7. Select the REM region and press ENTER.

8. For the base point, click near the lower-left corner of the REM region. For the second point, click in the upper-right corner, above the word Topographic, of the drawing as shown in the following illustration.

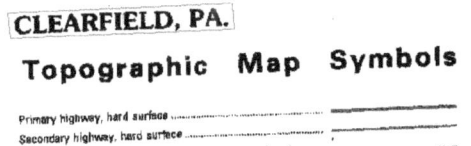

CLEARFIELD, PA.

Topographic Map Symbols

Primary highway, hard surface ....
Secondary highway, hard surface ....

9. In the Home tab, in the Modify panel, click Rotate.

10. Select the REM region and press ENTER.

11. Specify the rotation settings:
    - Click on the bottom-left corner of the REM region for the base point.
    - Enter **-2** as the rotation angle.
    - Press ENTER.

CLEARFIELD, PA.

Topographic Map Symbols

Primary highway, hard surface ....
Secondary highway, hard surface ....

12. In the Raster Tools tab, in the REM panel, click Merge to Raster Image.

13. Select the REM region and press ENTER.

Exercise: Copy a REM Region Across Two Drawings

In this exercise, you will create a REM region and copy it to another drawing. You will also scale and merge the REM region.

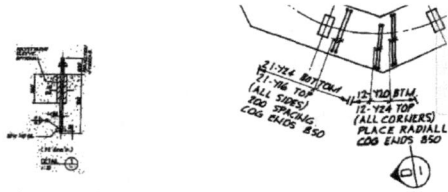

The completed exercise

1. Open ...\Editing Images Using Raster Entity Manipulation\Pedestal.dwg.

2. Open ...\Editing Images Using Raster Entity Manipulation\AB_detail.dwg.

3. In the View tab, in the Interface panel, click Tile Vertically. Both drawings are now visible.

4. Zoom to the extents of each drawing.

5. Click in the AB_detail.dwg to make it current, if it is not already current. In the Raster Tools tab, in the REM panel, expand the Create Region flyout and click Rectangular.

6. Draw a rectangle around the anchor bolt detail. It turns red.

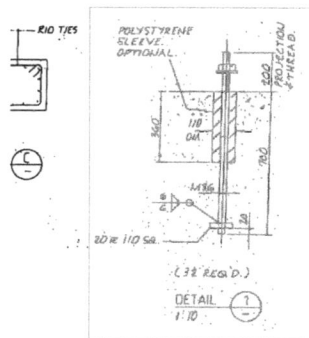

7. Select the frame of the REM region.

8. Hold the right mouse button and drag the REM region to Pedestal.dwg (near the left side of the detail). Release the mouse button when the REM region is inside the Pedestal drawing. In the shortcut menu, select Copy Here.

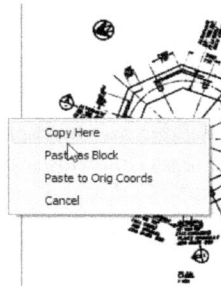

The new image is inserted into Pedestal.dwg. It might not be displayed because of the difference in the scales of the drawings.

9. Make the window with Pedestal.dwg active, if not already active, and Zoom to the extents of the drawing.

10. Select the REM region.

11. Scale the REM region (Click Dynamic Input to on):
    - Right-click on the region. Click Scale.
    - Specify the base point as **14,12**.
    - Enter **.001** to specify the scale factor.

12. Zoom to the extents of the image. The new image is placed along the bottom left corner of the drawing sheet.

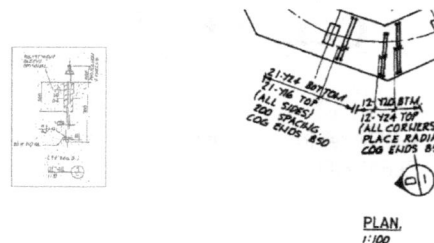

13. In the Raster Tools tab, in the REM panel, click Merge To Raster Image.

14. Pick the frame around the new REM region and press ENTER.

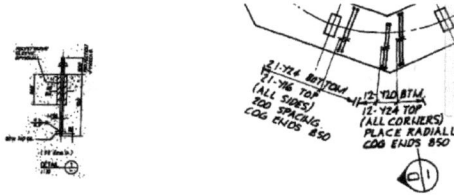

Lesson: Merging Vectors into Raster Images

Overview

In this lesson you learn the process of merging vector objects into raster images.

When your drawings incorporate both raster and vector information, you can use vector merge to create archive documents from these hybrid drawings.

Objectives

After completing this lesson, you will be able to:

- Identify the options used when merging vectors into raster images.
- Describe the cases in which you should merge vector and raster information.
- List the steps used to merge vectors into a raster image.
- Merge vectors into raster images.

About Merging Vectors

Merging vectors creates a raster equivalent of a vector object. When working with a hybrid drawing, you can merge vectors into an existing or new raster image.

You can only use the tools for merging vectors on one raster image at a time. If you have not selected an image, vector merge prompts you to create a new image to merge into.

Raster Pens

Using raster pens, you can thicken the lineweights of vector objects when you merge them into an image. Line widths or lineweights are assigned according to specified object colors.

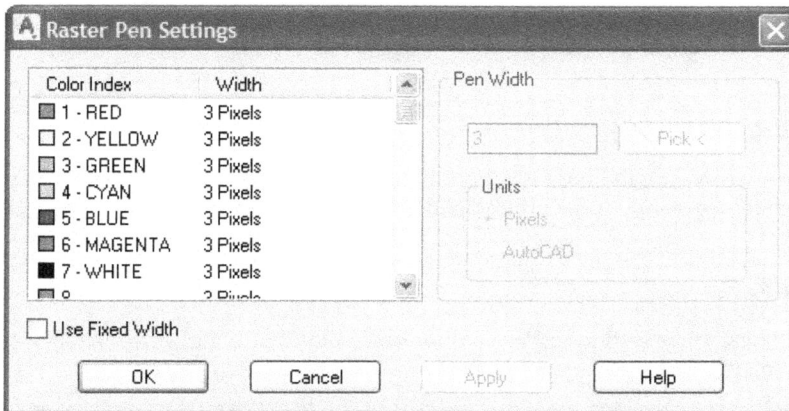

Setting raster pens before merging vectors is similar to setting a color-based plot-style table before plotting.

Example

You create a hybrid drawing by adding vector objects to a scanned document and want to merge them into a single drawing. By setting up raster pens before the merge, you can match the different line widths.

Hybrid Drawings and Merged Vectors

Guidelines for Merging Vectors

When you have a drawing that incorporates both raster and vector data, it is typically referred to as a hybrid drawing. You can usually save and print hybrid drawings easily. However, sometimes it is more effective to merge the vector data into the raster file.

- If you are using specific types of document management systems, they often cannot work with linked files or CAD data.
- You plan to send the file to someone who is not using a CAD system and cannot view the vector information.
- The information in the file is going to be posted to a website for viewing by the general public.
- The file is going to be incorporated in a report and the publishing software cannot read the CAD data.

Before Merging Vectors

Before you perform the vector merge, it is important to verify that the raster file format can support the information from the vectors. Check the color depth, resolution, and raster pen settings before merging.

About Raster Pens

Raster pens are similar to the settings used in a color-based plot style table. Note the following when setting up raster pens:

- You must click Apply after each change. Every change made to the raster pens is saved individually.
- Raster pens are applied based on the color of the vector entity.
- Raster pens can be set in pixels or AutoCAD drawing units.
- You can set a pen width by selecting points graphically.

Example

You are working on a remodeling project and the as-builts are only available as scans. You can insert the scanned plans into a new drawing and draw the proposed changes as vectors. If you need to save the plans back to a raster image for archiving purposes, you can use the vector merge tools.

Merging Vector Information Into a Raster Image

When you are merging vector information with raster data, it is important that you follow the steps in a specific order to ensure that the output matches your requirements. This section provides the steps to follow when performing a vector merge.

Procedure: Merging Vector and Raster Information

Use the following steps when merging vector objects into a raster image.

1. In the Raster Tools tab, in the expanded Edit panel, click Raster Pen.

2. In the Raster Pen Settings dialog box, select the colors used by the vector objects and set a pen width for the linework as it is going to be displayed in the raster image. Click OK.

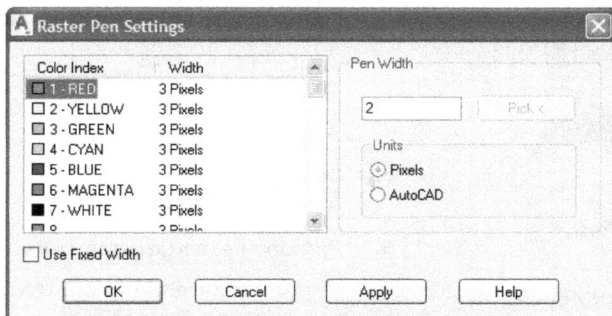

3. In the Raster Tools tab, in the expanded Edit panel, click Merge Vector.

4. Select the vectors and the raster image to be used for the merge in the same selection set. If there is only one image in the current drawing, it is automatically selected.

5. Select whether or not you want to remove the original vectors from the drawing. If you enter **No**, the vectors are merged into the raster image. However, they remain vectors in the current drawing.

Exercise: Merge Vectors

In this exercise, you will merge vector entities into a raster image.

The completed exercise

1. Open ...*Merging Vectors Into Raster Images\Deerorth.dwg*.

   If a Proxy Information dialog box opens, click OK.

2. In the Raster Tools tab, in the expanded Edit panel, click Raster Pen.

3. In the Raster Pen Settings dialog box, change the following pen widths:

   ■ Select Red. Under Pen Width, enter **2**. Click Apply.

   ■ Select Blue. Enter **4**. Click Apply.

   ■ Select Cyan. Enter **2**. Click Apply.

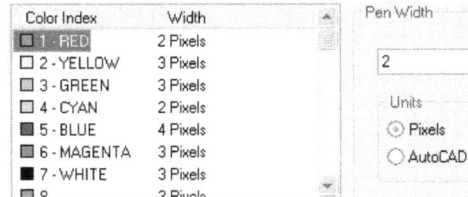

4. Click OK.

5. In the Raster Tools tab, in the expanded Edit panel, click Merge Vector.

6. Specify the merge parameters:

   ■ Select the entire image using a window selection. Press ENTER.

   ■ Press ENTER to delete the vector entities after the merge.

Chapter Summary

Having completed this chapter, you can:

- Clean up an image.
- Edit images using Raster Entity Manipulation.
- Merge vectors into raster images.

Working with DEM Data

This chapter introduces you to the concepts of working with digital elevation model (DEM) files, including how to insert them as images into a drawing and how to analyze them. DEM data is used in large-scale mapping and planning projects.

Objectives

After completing this chapter, you will be able to:

- Insert DEM data.
- Analyze DEM data.

Lesson: Inserting and Analyzing DEM Data

Overview

With the introduction of tools to work with digital elevation model (DEM) data, raster data can now be used as more than just a backdrop in mapping and GIS projects. You can now make better decisions for your projects by analyzing your raster data in creative ways while integrating it with existing vector project data. In this lesson you learn how to work with and analyze DEM files for site suitability analysis.

In the past, DEM data could only be manipulated in surface-modeling software that is targeted for the civil engineering and surveying professions. With the DEM tools provided in the AutoCAD® Raster Design software, anyone can create and display different interpretations of this data type.

Objectives

After completing this lesson, you will be able to:

- Identify a DEM file and its uses.
- Explain the concepts involved in working with a palette color map.
- Describe guidelines about working with DEM data.
- Acquire DEM data and prepare a drawing for its use.
- Insert a DEM.
- Create a palette color map.

What is a DEM?

Because DEM files are now considered raster images, new terms and concepts have been introduced. The definitions of the basic terms about DEM files are as follows.

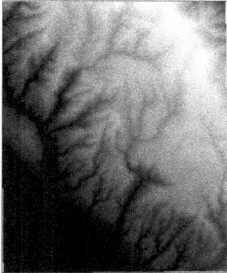

Digital Elevation Model

The digital elevation model (DEM) is a format for recording land elevations in an ASCII text-based file. A regular grid of survey points is created over a surface, and the elevation of each point is recorded as a floating-point number.

```
DEM GENERATED FROM 1/24,000 DLG-SOURCE, CI=40FT, PALO ALTO, CA, PROJ#1983, QD#08
0.000000000000000D+00    0.000000000000000D+00    0.000000000000000D-00    0.0
000000D-00    0.000000000000000D+00    0.000000000000000D+00    0.000000000000
0D-00    0.000000000000000D+00    2    2    4    0.577601296000000D+06    0
0D+07    0.588540457000000D+06    0.413673850300000D+07    0.588687560000000D+
0D-03    0.000000000000000D+00    10.300000E+02 0.300000E+02 0.100000E+01
+06    0.413367000000000D+07    0.000000000000000D-00    0.820000000000000D+02
```

Palette Color Map

A palette color map assigns colors to data values to provide a meaningful display of the contents of a file. It is used with a digital elevation model (DEM) to specify the display of surface elevations or slopes and to distribute a set of colors across a range of data values.

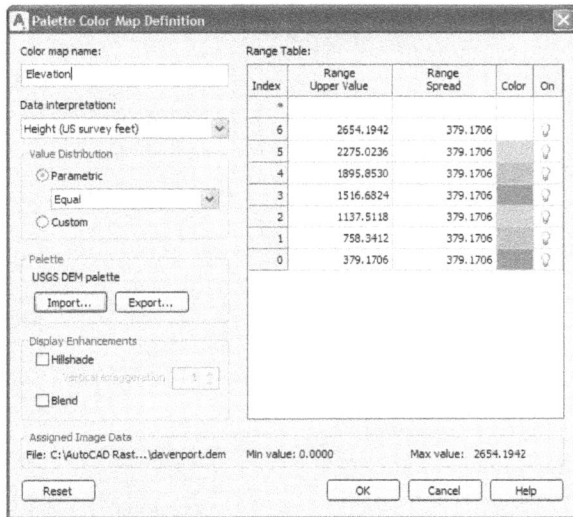

Example

When you are analyzing an area for elevation above sea level as part of a beach erosion study, you can import DEM files for two different dates and note how the shoreline areas have changed over time.

Using an elevation palette color map, you can highlight different ranges of elevations with different colors. Using a slope palette color map, you can verify the steepness of the beaches being studied.

Working with Palette Color Maps

Working with palette color maps, you can affect the data interpretation and value distribution.

Color map name: **Elevations**

Data interpretation: Height (US survey feet)

Value Distribution
- ( ) Parametric
  - Equal
- ( ) Custom

Palette
USGS DEM palette

[Import...] [Export...]

Display Enhancements
- [ ] Hillshade
  - Vertical exaggeration [1]
- [ ] Blend

Range Table:

Index	Range Upper Value	Range Spread	Color	On
*				
6	2654.1942	379.1706		
5	2275.0236	379.1706		
4	1895.8530	379.1706		
3	1516.6824	379.1706		
2	1137.5118	379.1706		
1	758.3412	379.1706		
0	379.1706	379.1706		

Assigned Image Data
File: C:\Autodesk Rast...\davenport.dem   Min value: 0.0000   Max value: 2654.1942

Data Interpretation

Data interpretation options control the type of data that is going to be displayed as extracted from the DEM file. These data types include height (in various units), slope, and direction of slope (also called aspect).

Data interpretation:

Value

- Height (US survey feet)
- Height (meters)
- Value
- Slope (Percent)
- Slope (Angle)
- Aspect

Value Distribution

The Value Distribution setting controls how the colors in the Range Table are distributed across the range of data values.

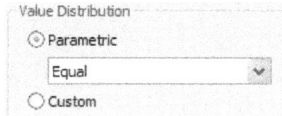

Palette File

A palette file is a simple ASCII file containing a header and up to 256 lines of information defining each shade in a palette color map. This information includes the number of ranges, distributions, and colors for each range. A palette file can be imported or exported into the Palette Color Map Definition dialog box. You can apply several standard palette files to new or existing palette color maps.

Example

You have a DEM file that is in meters and you want to analyze the data in a drawing that is set up to use feet as the base units. You can change the data interpretation type to switch the unit type used to display the elevations. By changing the data interpretation, you do not need to convert the DEM file.

Guidelines for Using DEM Data

The following are benefits of using the AutoCAD Raster Design software for DEM analysis.

- You are working directly with the DEM file. You do not need to convert the file or create a surface model based on the file. All of the displayed information is taken directly from the raw data and is not an interpolation of the data.
- You can easily change unit systems. By changing the data interpretation setting in the palette color map, you can display the DEM data in different unit systems, regardless of how the current drawing units are set. This is useful when you convert feet to meters or vice-versa.
- You can analyze different interpretations of the data without reimporting or recreating data files. Using the data interpretation setting in the palette color map, you can switch between viewing the DEM file as elevations or slopes.
- You can quickly create presentation pieces from the DEM file. Instead of going through a lengthy process of creating a surface model and creating displays of that model, you can directly set different range values and colors by adjusting the palette color map. Doing so immediately updates the display.
- You can import and export palette color maps to use with multiple DEM files or multiple projects. This ensures consistency between drawings.

Example

For the preliminary planning process on a parcel for a new development, you acquire DEM data for the area and use the tools in the AutoCAD Raster Design software to check the elevation and slope for site suitability. This data can also be used to set up a preliminary hydrology study to determine runoff areas and slopes.

Preparing to Use DEM Data

Acquiring DEM Files

To acquire DEM files, use the following sources:

Source	Description
Federal Government	Many agencies provide DEM files to the public. They can be downloaded from a website or purchased on CD.
Local Government	Many local government agencies have information as part of GIS or asset management systems that can include DEM files. Occasionally, these are data files that have been collected from a federal agency and made available to the local public.
Universities and Other Secondary Educational Institutions	Large educational institutions often collect data (usually of local interest) as part of research projects. This data is sometimes made available, especially in the case of publicly funded institutions.

Procedure: Setting Up a Drawing for Use with DEM Files

1. Acquire the DEM files and verify the location and unit types.

2. Set the units for the current drawing.

3. Verify that any vector or other raster components of the drawing represent the same area as the DEM file.

4. If you are working with a custom palette color map that was created for another DEM file. Verify that is has been exported to an accessible location. You can then import and reuse the palette color map, rather than creating a new one from scratch.

5. Set a layer for the DEM file.

Inserting DEM Files

You can insert DEM files into the current drawing and manage them with the tools that you also use with other raster image file formats. When inserting DEM files, note the following points:

- You can insert multiple DEM files at the same time. All files that are inserted at the same time use the same palette color map.

- In the Raster Tools tab, in the Manage & View panel, click Manage... to open the Image Manager as shown in the following illustration. You can use it to display information about a previously inserted DEM file.

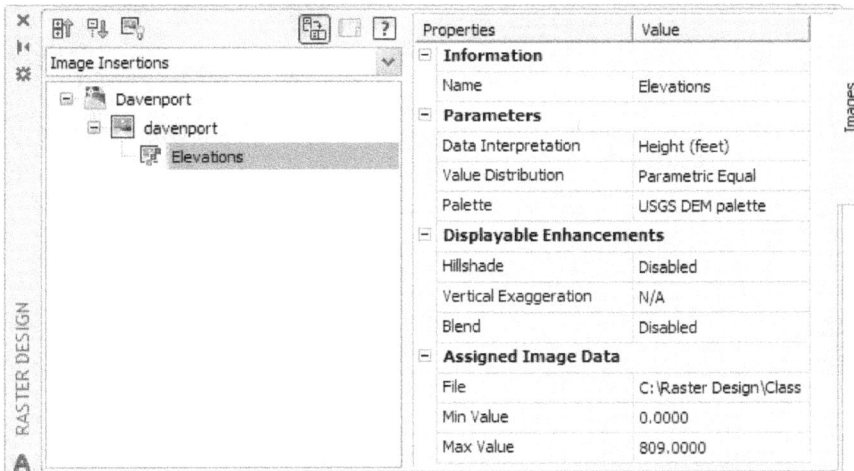

Exercise: Insert a DEM

In this exercise, you will insert a DEM file into a drawing. You will then select how to display this file by selecting a palette color map using the Image Insertion wizard.

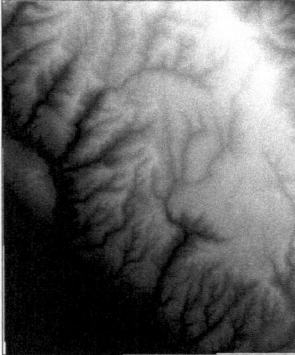

The completed exercise

1. Open ...\Inserting and Analyzing DEM Data\ DEM_1.dwg.

2. In the Raster Tools tab, in the Insert & Write panel, click Insert.

3. In the Insert Image dialog box, select ...\Inserting and Analyzing DEM Data\ davenport.dem.

4. In the Insert Options area, select Insertion wizard and Zoom to image(s). Click Open.

5. In the Assign Color Map dialog box, verify that Color map is set to Standard and that Insert into display is checked.

6. Click Next in the rest of the pages in the wizard. Click Finish in the last page.

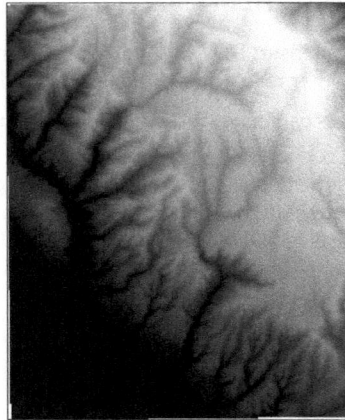

Exercise: Create a Palette Color Map

In this exercise, you will create a new palette color map and apply it to an existing DEM file.

The completed exercise

1. Open ...*Inserting and Analyzing DEM Data\Davenport.dwg*.

2. In the Raster Tools tab, in the Manage & View panel, click Manage.

3. Select the Image Insertions view.

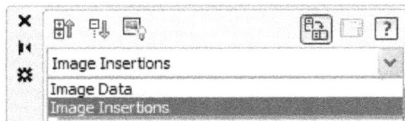

4. Click Expand Tree.

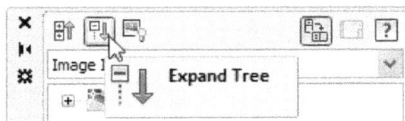

5. Right-click on the Standard palette color map. Click Edit Color Map.

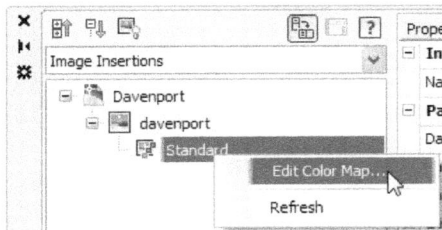

6. In the Palette Assignment Color Map dialog box, click Create new color map.

7. In the Palette Color Map Definition dialog box.

   - For Color map name, enter **Elevations**.
   - For Data interpretation, select Height (US survey feet).
   - Under Value Distribution, verify that Parametric is set as Equal.

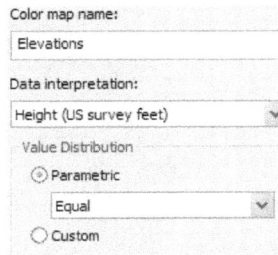

8. In the Palette area, click Import. In the Import Palette dialog box, select *USGS_DEM.pf*. Click Open.

9. Click OK to close the Palette Color Map Definition dialog box. Click OK to close the Palette Assignment Color Map dialog box.

10. Close the Image Manager.

Chapter Summary

Having completed this chapter, you can:

- Insert DEM data.
- Analyze DEM data.

Raster to Vector Conversion

This chapter shows you how to convert raster data into vector entities. You can use the vectorization tools manually or semi-automatically to convert text into a raster image to text entities or to export text to a word processing or spreadsheet software.

Objectives

After completing this chapter, you will be able to:

- Use vectorization tools for interactive conversion.
- Use vectorization line-following tools.
- Create contours using the Contour Follower.
- Convert text.

Lesson: Using Vectorization Tools for Interactive Conversion

Overview

In this lesson you learn how to convert raster lines, rectangles, circles, and arcs into vectors and how to replace selected raster elements in an image with vectors. The vectorization tools help you to draw precise vector geometry that traces the raster linework in an image. You can use the vectorization tools to interactively convert entire raster images into vector.

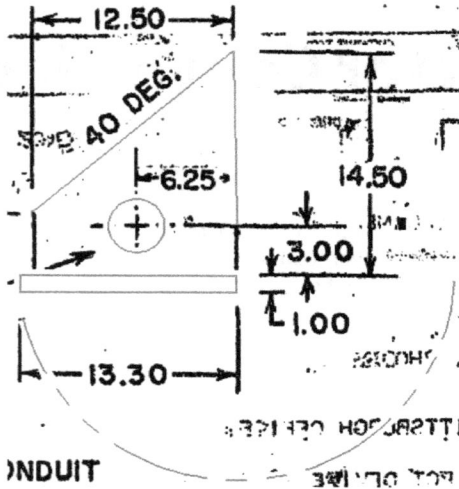

Sometimes you need vector drawings rather than raster background images, such as when you are generating 3D designs, reusing design elements, or making major changes to a design. VTools help you to convert your raster drawings while preserving the accuracy of the design.

Objectives

After completing this lesson, you will be able to:

- Define the terms used in interactive vectorization.
- Determine when to convert raster into vector.
- Identify VTools options and best practices.
- Convert raster into vector using VTools.

About Vectorization

Vectorization is the process of converting a raster image into vector objects. However, using the vectorization tools in the AutoCAD® Raster Design software, you can only convert elements of a bitonal image.

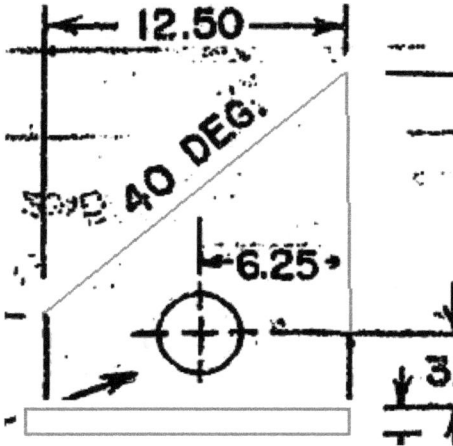

Interactive Conversion

In the process of interactive conversion, you manually convert a bitonal raster arc, circle, line, or rectangle into its equivalent vector object. As part of this process, you can review the properties of the new vector entities, such as length, radius, and angle, and make any required modifications.

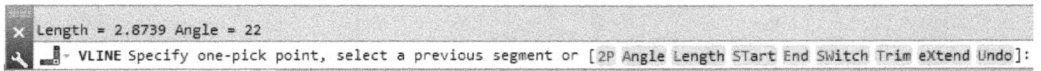

```
Length = 2.8739 Angle = 22
- VLINE Specify one-pick point, select a previous segment or [2P Angle Length STart End SWitch Trim eXtend Undo]:
```

Raster Snap

The Raster Snap options enable you to snap the cursor to the end, center, corner, intersection, or edge points on a bitonal raster entity. If you select more than one snap mode, the crosshairs snap to the closest of the possible snap points. When the crosshairs snap to a point that you want to use, select the point. You can set the options in the Raster Tools tab, in the Snap panel or in the Raster Snap tab, in the Drafting Settings dialog box, as shown in the following illustration.

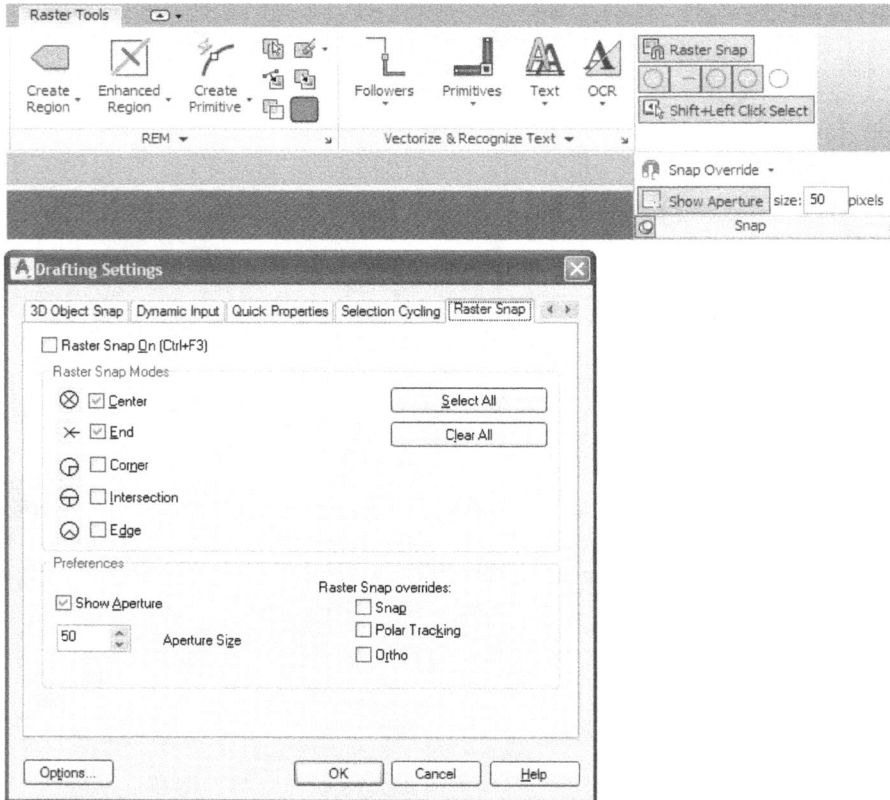

Raster snap modes are similar to the AutoCAD® Osnap options for vector entities.

Example

You want to use the lot lines on a scanned parcel map as the base for a new development. You can use VTools to only convert the lot lines to vector lines and to save them in a separate drawing file.

For minor edits, you can use the Raster Entity Manipulation (REM) editing tools rather than converting an entire image to vectors.

Vectorization Versus Raster Editing

The AutoCAD Raster Design software has tools for raster editing and vectorization. Each type of tool is used in for different conditions. The VTools in the AutoCAD Raster Design software enable you to manually convert elements of a scanned drawing to their equivalent vector entities and to edit the new entities to create different designs.

The raster editing tools, such as those used in REM, enable you to directly edit portions of a raster image without having to convert them into vectors. Use the following guidelines to determine when each type of process is applicable.

Guidelines for Vectorization Versus Raster Editing

Use vectorization in the following situations:

- You are using the drawing elements repeatedly, often with minor variations.
- You need to create 3D models from the design.
- You need the drawing elements for further design and analysis.
- You need to export design elements to other drafting, modeling, design, or manufacturing software.

Use raster editing in the following situations:

- You are reproducing a design with a few, minor changes.
- You need to copy or move drawing elements without any other edits.
- You need to remove elements of a drawing before printing.
- You want to draw attention to one portion of an image (such as an inset), or add color to a portion of a grayscale image.

Vectorizing an Image

Note the following when vectorizing an image:

- The vectorization process can be time-consuming. Verify that you really need the drawing elements to be vectors. Some edits are easier to perform on the raster data.
- Vectorization only works on bitonal images. If you need to copy a portion of a grayscale or color image, (such as an aerial photograph), use REM, which works with any image type.

There are situations in which using either vectorization or raster editing tools provides the equivalent results in the same amount of time. However, in most cases using the raster editing tools is preferable.

Example

Vectorization is the best tool to use when:

- You want to use a scanned contour map to create a surface model.
- A floor plan is used to create a 3D building model.
- A mechanical part is going to be prototyped with a multiaxis milling machine.
- An electrical schematic is partially redesigned.

Vectorization Options

You can use the following options with vectorization to increase the accuracy and speed of the process:

- Raster Snaps.
- The Raster Entity Detection tab in the AutoCAD Raster Design Options dialog box.
- The VTools General tab in the AutoCAD Raster Design Options dialog box.

Each of these tools has specific uses and setting the options correctly greatly increases productivity.

Raster Snap Options

Using Raster Snaps enables you to select points more accurately in a bitonal image. This is similar to using Osnaps to select points on vector entities.

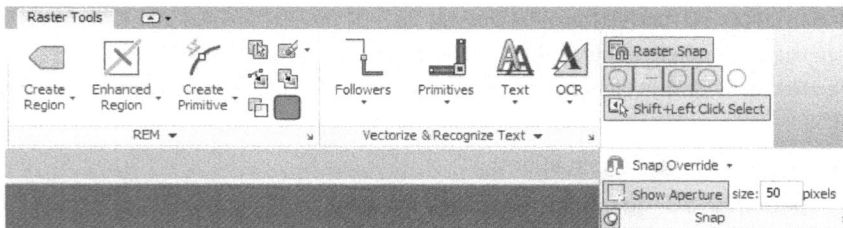

AutoCAD Raster Entity Detection Options

The AutoCAD Raster Entity Detection settings control how the AutoCAD Raster Design software recognizes which raster elements are part of the linework to be converted. This includes recognizing linework with gaps (such as contour lines or poorly scanned drawings), and noncontinuous linework, (such as dashed or dotted linetypes).

The settings in the Raster Entity Detection tab, in the AutoCAD Raster Design Options dialog box, are shown in the following illustration.

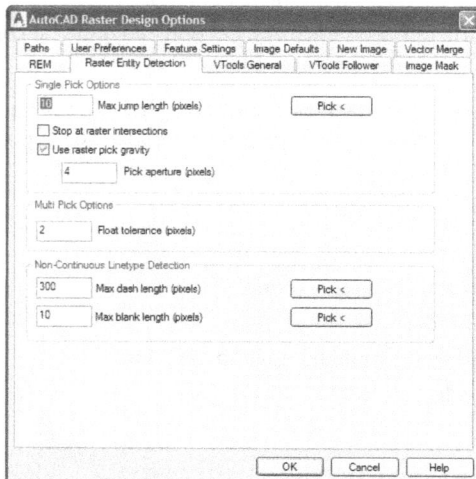

VTools General Options

The VTools General options control how the vector geometry is created and what happens to the raster. This includes how to remove the underlying raster information and how to use shortcut menus to help verify object properties. The settings in the VTools General tab in the AutoCAD Raster Design Options dialog box, are shown in the following illustration.

Preparing to Use VTools

Before vectorizing the image, use the following steps:

1. Verify that the image is bitonal. If not, use the Change Color Depth tool to convert it to Bitonal.

2. Use the AutoCAD Raster Design Options dialog box to verify that all of the settings are correct.

3. Check the raster snaps to verify that they have been set correctly.

4. Verify that a layer has been set for the new vector data. All vectors are placed on the current layer unless you are using the Vector Separation options in the VTools General tab.

Example

You are using a scan of a fairly degraded drawing and some of the linework is broken. Use the Max jump length setting in the Raster Entity Detection tab in the AutoCAD Raster Design Options dialog box so that VTools interprets the elements as complete lines, arcs, or circles

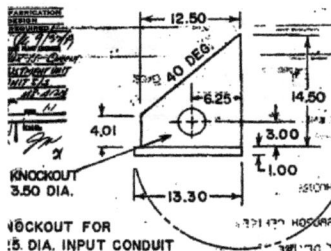

Exercise: Convert Raster to Vector with VTools

In this exercise you will convert raster elements in an image into vector geometry using the AutoCAD Raster Design VTools.

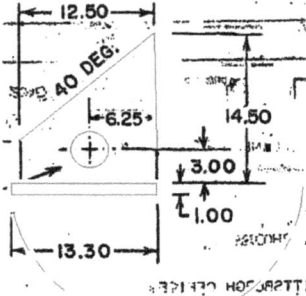

The completed exercise

1. Open ...\Using Vectorization Tools for Interactive Conversion\Document.dwg.

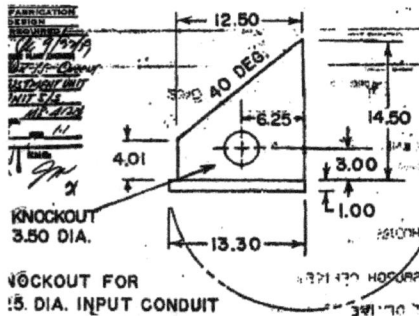

2. In the Raster Tools tab, in the lower right corner of Insert & Write panel, click the Options arrow.

3. In the AutoCAD Raster Design Options dialog box, click the Feature Settings tab. For the Rub / Crop Line Width, enter **0.75**.

4. Click OK.

5. In the Raster Tools tab, in the Snap panel, click Raster Snap to toggle it on, if required.

6. In the Snap panel, click End, Corner, and Intersection snap modes.

   Note: Open the Drafting Settings dialog box by clicking the arrow in the right corner of the Snap panel and select the required Raster Snap Modes.

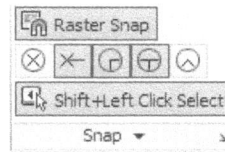

7. Verify that ORTHOMODE is off.

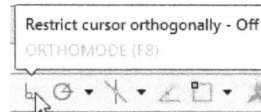

8. In the Raster Tools tab, in the Vectorize & Recognize Text panel, expand Primitives and click Line.

9. Specify the parameters as follows:

   - Enter **2P** for the 2 Point method.
   - Zoom to the 40 DEG area in the image. Select points 1, 2, and 3 shown in the following illustration.

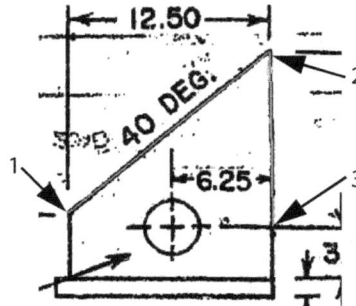

10. Press ENTER to complete the line and exit the command.

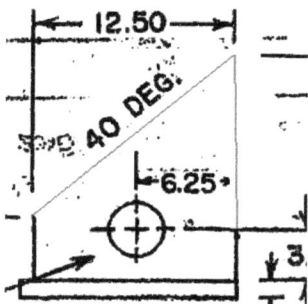

11. In the Raster Tools tab, in the Vectorize & Recognize Text panel, expand Primitives and click Rectangle.

12. Define the rectangle as follows:

- Pick the top-left corner of the rectangle representing the base of the figure with the lines just created.
- Press ENTER to accept the angle default of 0.
- Pick the lower-right corner of the rectangle for the other corner point.
- Press ENTER.

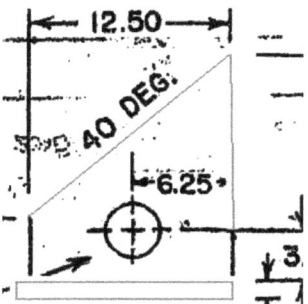

13. In the Raster Tools tab, in the Vectorize & Recognize Text panel, expand Primitives and click Circle.

14. Specify the Circle settings as follows:

- Enter **C** to pick the center of the circle. Pick the circle center.
- Pick a point on the circumference of the circle to specify the radius.
- Press ENTER to complete the command.

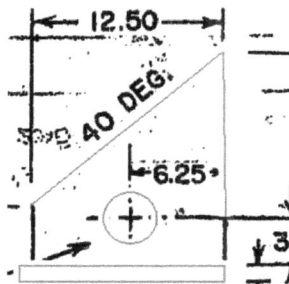

15. Make the layer DIM the current layer.

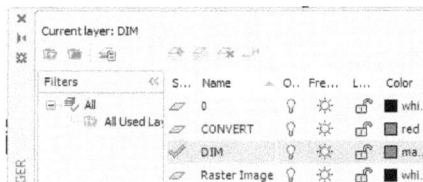

16. In the Raster Tools tab, in the Vectorize & Recognize Text panel, expand Primitives and click Arc. Define the arc as follows:

- Enter **3P** for the 3 Point option.
- Use the following illustration to select the points 1, 2, and 3.

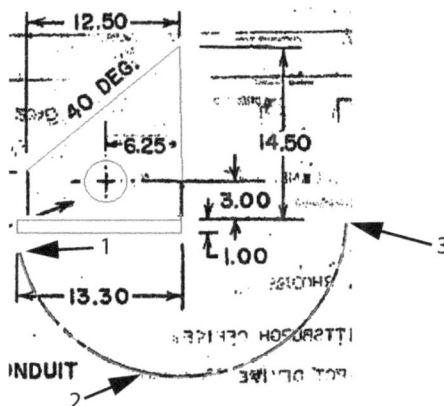

17. Press ENTER to complete the arc.

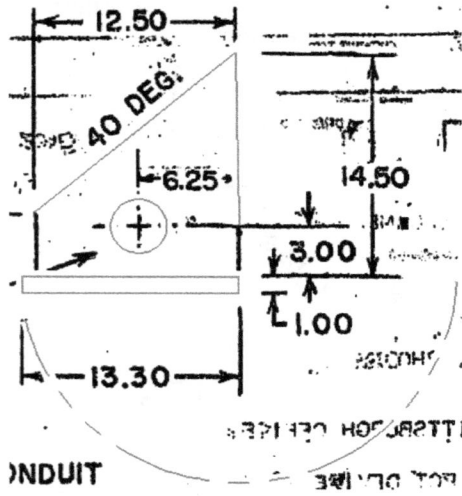

Lesson: Using Vectorization Line Following Tools

Overview

In this lesson you learn how to use the tools and options that are available for converting raster data into vector data using semiautomatic line following.

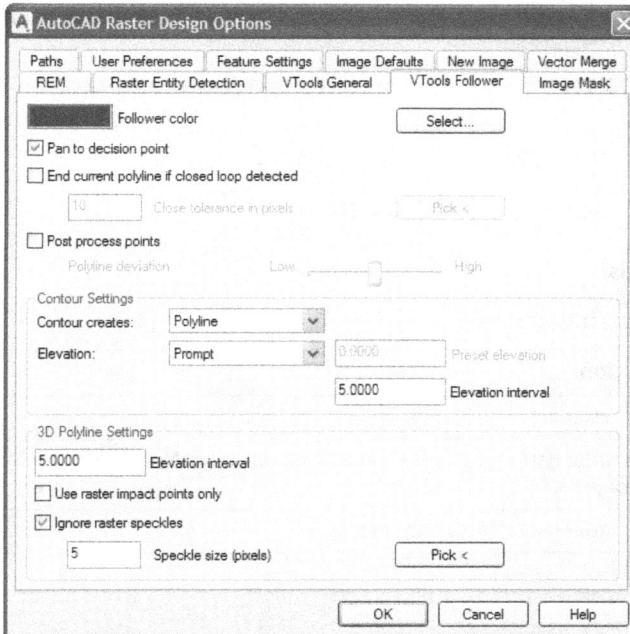

Line-following tools can dramatically increase conversion speed when you convert complex geometry, such as topographic maps and electrical wiring diagrams, into polylines for use in other designs.

Objectives

After completing this lesson, you will be able to:

- Define the terms used with line-following vectorization tools.
- Describe the line-following command options.
- Use line-following commands to convert portions of a raster image into vector entities.

About Vectorization Line-Following Tools

VTools Follower

VTools Follower (also called a line follower), traces raster lines in a bitonal image and creates vectors (polylines) that are recognized by the AutoCAD software as individual objects.

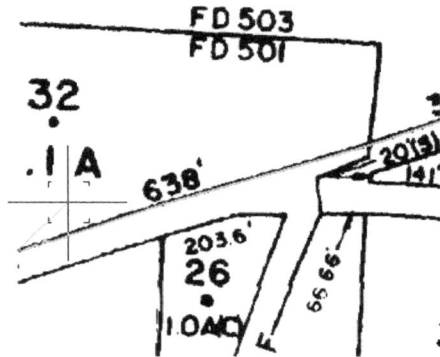

Line Following Commands

The three VTools followers are described as follows:

Command	Description
Polyline Follower	Converts raster data into 2D polylines.
Contour Follower	Converts raster data into 2D polylines with elevations or AutoCAD® Land Desktop contour objects.
3D Polyline Follower	Converts raster data into 3D polylines.

Command Line Options

Options for the line-following tools display in the Command Line and can be used when lines are being converted.

Example

You plan to scan a street map and incorporate it into a GIS database. If you convert the street right-of-ways into polyline boundaries using the polyline follower, you can use them for GIS identification.

Line Following Options

VTools Follower Options

A number of options that control the line-following tools are located in the VTools Follower tab in the AutoCAD Raster Design Options dialog box.

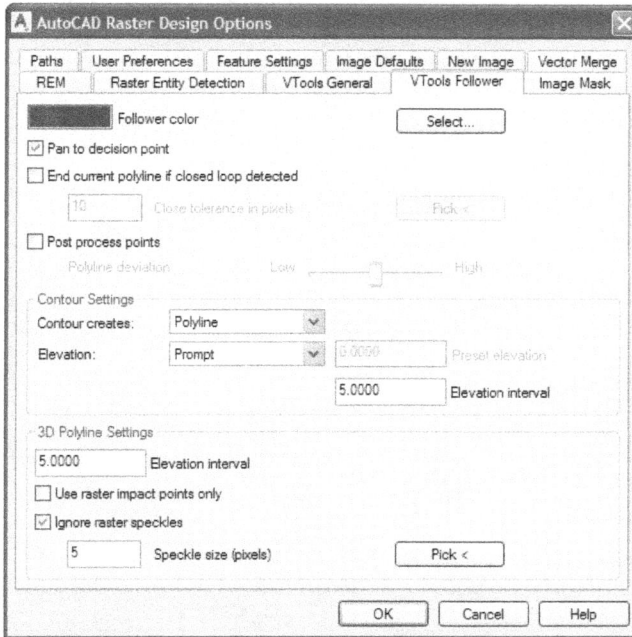

Three categories of options are available. Four options can be used with all of the follower commands, but the others are specific to the Contour or 3D Polyline followers.

Option	Description
Follower Color	Displays the current color used to mark the progress of the follower. Click Select to open the color palette.
Pan to Decision Point	When the path for the line follower is not clear (such as at an intersection), the follower automatically pans to ensure that the current decision point is always displayed.
End Current Polyline If Closed Loop Detected	Closes polylines automatically when the endpoints are within the tolerance distance. This is useful for closing across labels in contour lines.

Additionally, all of the VTools Followers respect the settings in the Raster Entity Detection and VTools General tabs in the AutoCAD Raster Design Options dialog box.

Guidelines for Using the Line Following Tools

When you use the line-following tools, note the following:

- Set the options before using the line following commands.
- Line following tools only work on binary images.
- Although you can only follow linework on one image at a time, you can join separate polylines after they have been created.
- Use the Command Line options to correct following errors on the fly or to modify the results of the line following.

VTools Follower Options

Many of the VTools followers options are available in the Command Line as shown in the following illustration.

```
Command:
Specify point to follow or [manually Add/Partial]:
⌐ ⌐ VFPLINE Manually add point or [Add Switch Backup Rollback Direction cOntinue Vector Close Join]:
```

These options and their functions are as follows:

Option	Description
Add	Manually adds a point to the polyline.
Switch	Switches between decision points.
Backup	Goes back to the previous vertex.
Rollback	Backs up to a selected vertex.
Direction	Indicates a direction to follow when there is a decision point.
Continue	Maintains the current direction of the follower. You must enter **O** in the Command Line to use this option.
Vector	Specifies the first and last vertices of a vector to follow, rather than the raster.
Close	Closes the polyline by drawing a single segment between the first and last points.
Join	Joins an existing vector polyline to the current polyline.

Exercise: Convert Raster to Vector with the Polyline Follower

In this exercise, you will set options for converting raster data using the polyline follower and convert a right-of-way line from a scanned topo map into a vector polyline.

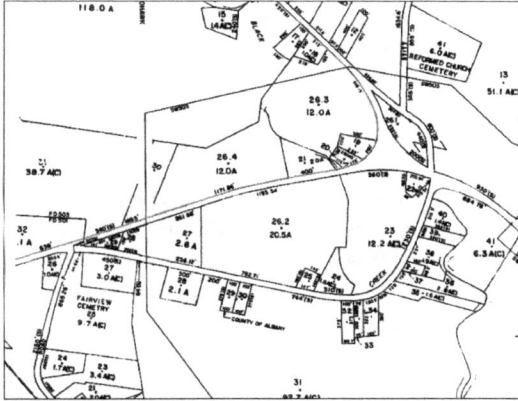

The completed exercise

1. Open ...\Using the Vectorization Line Following Tools\Topo Map.dwg.

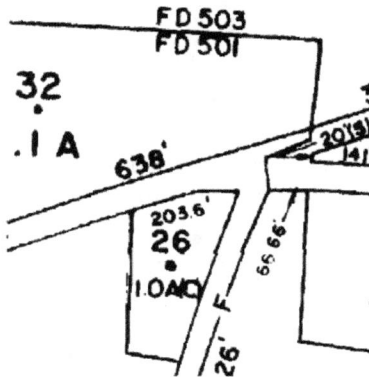

2. In the Raster Tools tab, in the lower right corner of a panel, click the Options arrow. The AutoCAD Raster Design Options dialog box opens.

3. Click the VTools Follower tab.

4. Click Select.

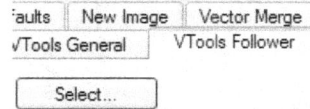

5. In the Select Color dialog box, click the green color swatch. Click OK.

6. Verify that the Pan to decision point check box is selected. Verify that the End current polyline if closed loop detected check box is cleared.

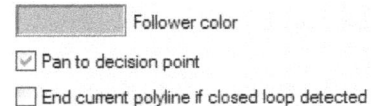

7. Click OK.

8. In the Raster Tools tab, in the Vectorize & Recognize Text panel, expand Followers and click Polyline Follower.

9. Click the top right-of-way line.

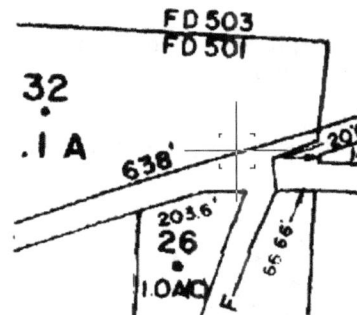

10. The polyline follower reaches the left edge of the line. Enter **S** and then press ENTER to switch to the opposite end of the new polyline.

11. Note that the polyline has followed the wrong path, making a turn at the lot line between Lots 17 and 18.

Enter **R** and press ENTER to return to a previous point on the line.

12. Click the right-of-way line (along the edge of lot 18) just before the polyline begins to follow the lot line.

13. Click the right-of-way line just inside Lot 17.

14. Enter **O,** press ENTER to continue following the right-of-way line.

15. Press ENTER to finish the line when the polyline follower reaches the edge of the image. Press ENTER to finish the command.

16. Zoom to the extents of the drawing to display the new right-of-way vector polyline.

Lesson: Creating Contours Using the Contour Follower

Overview

In this lesson you learn how to convert contours and set options to make the process more efficient. Using this process you can convert contours, such as those in scanned topo maps, to polylines with elevations or to contour objects. Converting contours is almost identical to using the VTools polyline follower.

Contours are often used as the base for a surface model. When you convert scanned topo maps into contours with true elevations, you can use them to create surface models and cut profiles, to determine the elevation at selected points, and to perform other types of surface analysis.

Objectives

After completing this lesson, you will be able to:

- Define the terms used when converting contour maps.
- Describe the different types of contour data that can be generated using the Contour Follower.
- Identify the preparations that should be made before converting contours.
- Create contours using the contour follower.

Converting Contour Maps

Although the process is almost identical to that of using the VTools polyline follower, contour conversion uses the following additional settings and terms.

About Contour Following Options

As with the polyline follower, the contour follower is controlled by the option settings in the VTools General and VTools Follower tabs in the AutoCAD Raster Design Options dialog box. Two additional options only affect the contour follower.

Option	Description
Contour Creates	Controls whether the contour follower creates polylines or contour objects.
Elevation	Controls how elevations are assigned to the contours and any default settings for elevations.

You can also use vector separation to assign layers to the new contours.

Contour Elevation Interval

To create a suggested elevation value when you create contours, you can use the contour elevation interval to specify the amount that is added or subtracted from the last elevation value that was entered. This setting is located in the AutoCAD Raster Design Options dialog box.

Vector Separation

When creating vectors, use vector separation to control how tools assign line widths and layers.

Example

When converting a large contour map, you can use the vector separation settings to preset the layers on which the new contours are going to be placed. You can have the default elevations display at the prompt line by setting a contour elevation interval. If the elevation interval is set correctly, when the elevation for the first contour is entered, you can press ENTER to accept the default elevation for all of the subsequent contours.

It is easier to use the contour follower with a preset interval and vector separation than it is to convert the contours to polylines using the polyline follower and then change the layers and elevations manually.

Types of Contour Data

When converting contours, you can display them as contour objects or polylines.

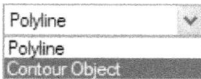

Polyline	∨
Polyline	
Contour Object	

Contour Data Types

The following types of contour data can be created using the contour follower.

Data Type	Description
Polyline	When the contour follower creates polylines, they are 2D AutoCAD polylines. The polyline width can be set using the vector separation options, and the polyline elevation can be set using the Elevation option in the VTools Follower tab in the AutoCAD Raster Design Options dialog box.
Contour Object	Contour objects are only available when you are using the AutoCAD Raster Design software in conjunction with the AutoCAD Land Desktop software. They are true objects with an inherent elevation property. The appearance of contour objects is controlled by contour styles that are set in the AutoCAD Land Desktop software.

The advantages of using contour objects rather than polylines are as follows:

- A smaller drawing size than the polyline representation of a contour.
- A context-sensitive shortcut menu that can be opened by right-clicking.
- Better listing capabilities. Only the information that is relevant to each AEC contour displays, such as elevation and layer, rather than displaying a listing for every contour vertex.
- Dynamic labeling that automatically updates the label when you edit the contour.
- Better display control. When using DVIEW twist to adjust the view orientation of a drawing, the contour label remains upright.
- More intuitive editing. If you delete a label, the gap in the contour is eliminated.

Preparing a Contour Map for Conversion

When you convert contours from a scanned map, use the following steps before using the contour follower to ensure accurate output.

Procedure: Preparing a Contour Map for Conversion

Use the following steps before using the contour follower.

1. Verify that the image is bitonal (black and white). If not, use the Change Color Depth or Histogram tools to convert the image. If you are using a palette color image, such as a USGS quad sheet, you can use the Palette Manager to isolate the color used for contours, and then the Histogram tool to convert it to a bitonal image.

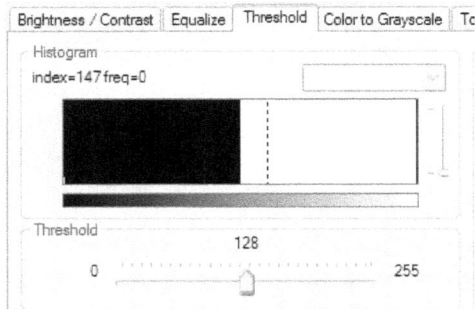

2. Verify that the resolution of the image is 300 dpi. If not, use the Change Resolution tool to convert it.

3. If the contours shown in the raster image are difficult to follow, use the Bitonal Filters to enhance the image.

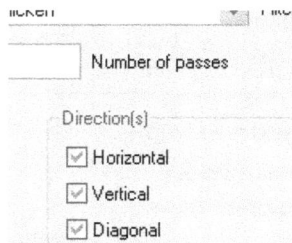

4. Use the Raster Entity Detection tab in the AutoCAD Raster Design Options dialog box to control how the contour follower recognizes gaps and dashed lines.

5. Use the VTools General tab in the AutoCAD Raster Design Options dialog box to control vector separation.

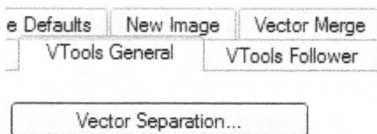

6. Use the VTools Follower tab in the AutoCAD Raster Design Options dialog box to select the type of object to be created and any elevation preferences.

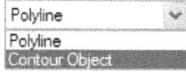

| Polyline ▾ |
| Polyline |
| Contour Object |

Contour-Following Guidelines

Note the following when using the contour follower:

- You can only convert binary images.
- You can only convert contours from one image at a time.
- You can convert portions of a contour line using the Partial option.

Exercise: Create Contours Using the Contour Follower

In this exercise, you will create contours from an existing scanned topo map and set the options required to convert this map with a minimal amount of effort.

The completed exercise

1. Open ...\Creating Contours Using the Contour Follower\Contour Map.dwg.

2. In the Raster Tools tab, in the lower right corner of a panel, click the Options arrow. The AutoCAD Raster Design Options dialog box opens.

3. Click VTools General tab.

4. Click Vector Separation.

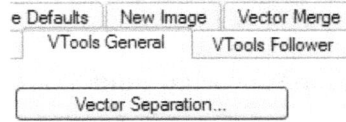

5. In the Vector Separation Options dialog box, click the Contour tab.

6. Under Minor, for Interval, enter **10**. For Layer, select CONT-10.

   Under Major, for Interval, enter **50**. For Layer, select CONT-50.

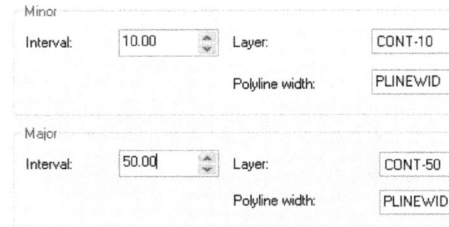

7. Click OK.

8. Click the VTools Follower tab.

9. Use the following settings:

   - Select the End current polyline if closed loop detected check box.
   - Under Contour Settings, for Elevation interval, enter **10**.

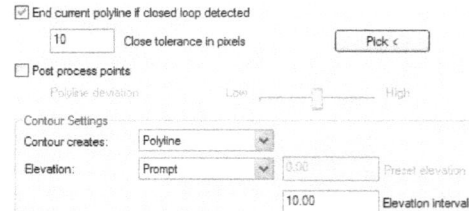

10. Click OK.

11. In the Raster Tools tab, in the Vectorize & Recognize Text tab, expand the Followers flyout and click Contour Follower.

12. Click the 90 contour as shown in the following illustration.

13. Enter **90**. Press ENTER.

14. Click the 100 contour. Enter **C** to close the contour loop. Press ENTER to use an elevation of 100.

15. Press ENTER to end the command.

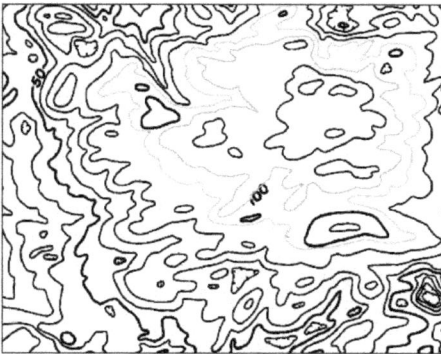

Lesson: Converting Text

Overview

In this lesson you learn how to convert text from a scanned image to AutoCAD text entities or external files.

Just as you use vectorization tools to convert scanned linework to AutoCAD vector entities, you can use the text recognition tools to extract scanned text as AutoCAD text objects for use in your current drawing.

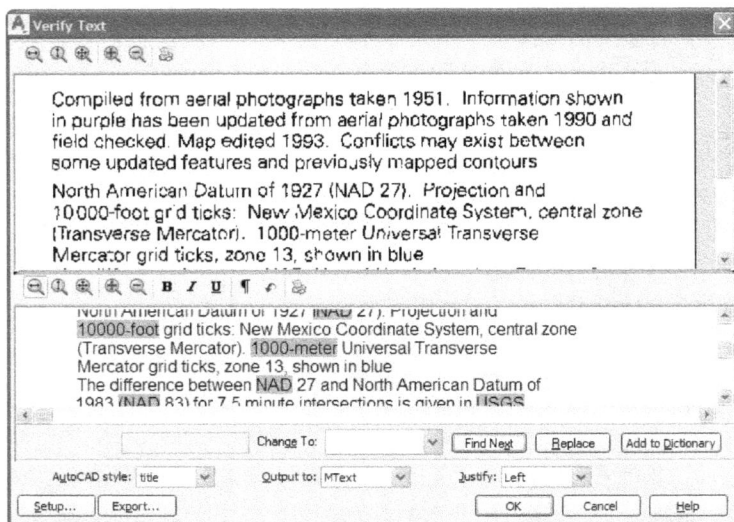

Objectives

After completing this lesson, you will be able to:

- Identify different types of scanned text.
- Determine when text should be converted and the best techniques to use.
- Prepare for converting text from a scanned image.

About Converting Text

You typically use text conversion on blocks of text that you need to reuse or edit. The following definitions introduce the concepts and define the terms involved in converting text.

Optical Character Recognition

Optical character recognition (OCR) determines which letter, number, or punctuation mark is represented by a connected series of pixels in a raster image and used by the tools in the Text Recognition menu.

Standard Text

Text that represents labels, sentences, or paragraphs is treated as standard text and can be converted to AutoCAD Text or Mtext entities. Construction notes, callouts, and specifications are considered standard text. Standard text can also be exported to an external text file. It is converted using the Recognize Text tool.

NOTES

1) *(+12") DENOTES EXISTING SUPPORTS SHALL BE EXTENDED AS SHOWN ON DETAIL 'D1' ON DWG LENGTH IN BRACKETS DENOTES LENGTH REQUIRED.

2) ALL SAFETY SYSTEM PANS (KL&M) SHALL BE HEAVY DUTY 4 3/4" DEEP&SOLID COVERS. ALL OTHER PANS TO BE LADDER TYPE.

Before

NOTES

1) *(+12")DENOTES EXISTING SUPPORTS SHALL BE EXTENDED AS SHOWN ON DETAIL 'D1' ON DWG LENGTH IN BRACKETS DENOTES LENGTH REQUIRED.

2) ALL SAFETY SYSTEM PANS (KL&M) SHALL BE HEAVY DUTY 4 3/4" DEEP SOLID COVERS. ALL OTHER PANS TO BE LADDER TYPE.

After

Table Text

Text organized into a schedule or chart is treated as table text and can only be converted into individual AutoCAD Text entities. Door schedules and curve tables are considered table text. Table text can also be exported to an external spreadsheet file. It is converted using the Recognize Table tool.

window, door, lintel, schedule

Window door	Boulton & Paul ref N°	Catric lintel ref N° and length
W1	212C	CN7E 1.500
W2	109C	CN7E 0.930
W3	3N10CC	CN7F 1.642
W4	210C	CN7E 1.500
W5	310CC	CN7F 2.070
W6	207C	CN7E 1.500
01	—	CN7E 1.200
PD1	—	CN7A 2.400

Before

window, door, lintel, schedule

Window door	Boulton & Paul ref No.	Catric lintel ref No and length
W1	212C	CN7E 1.500
W2	109C	CN7E 0.930
W3	3N10CC	CN7e 1.642
W4	210C	CN7E 1.500
W5	310CC	CN7F 2.070
W6	207C	CN7E 1.500
01	–	CN7E 1.200
PD1	–	CN7A 2.400

After

Text Verification

Text verification reviews the results of a raster-to-vector text conversion. Because no text recognition engine is completely accurate, it is very important that you review the results before inserting them into a drawing or exporting them to an external file.

Using the text verification screen, you can check the results of the conversion and make any required edits. The Verify Text and Verify Table dialog boxes are divided into two panes, which display the original raster information and the conversion results. Text that does not match the selected dictionaries is highlighted.

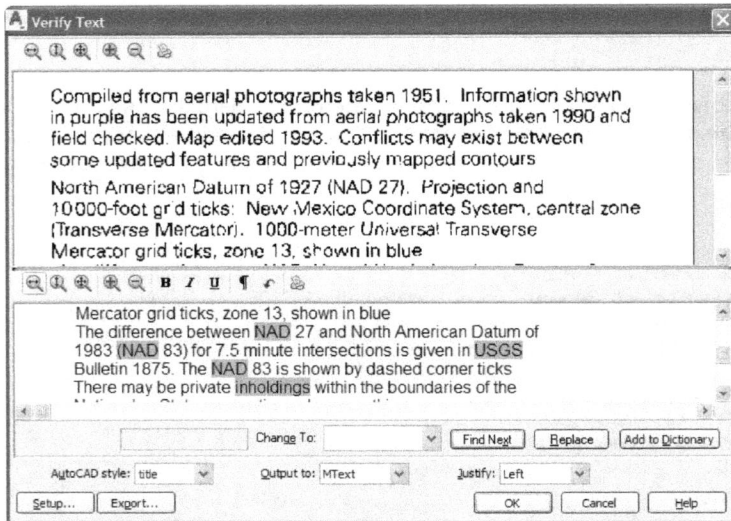

Example

For example, you want to convert construction notes scanned from an archive print to vector AutoCAD text entities for use in new project with only minor edits. You can do so using the Recognize Text tool, which creates standard text. You would not use the Recognize Table tool because construction notes are rarely in tabular form.

Text Conversion Principles

When you work with scanned drawings, you can edit the linework (such as arcs, circles, and lines), using tools in the AutoCAD Raster Design software. Text in a raster form cannot be edited or manipulated easily. Therefore, you can use the text recognition tools when you need to change text or extract it from a drawing for use in other applications.

When to Convert Text

Using text recognition tools can make the drafting or design process faster in the following situations:

- Create a new set of drawings using an existing set. Many notes and schedules can be used with minor content edits.
- Converting text that is going to be used repeatedly in future projects. Specifications and construction notes are frequently used in multiple projects with little variation.
- Extracting information from a scanned drawing, such as project names or job numbers for cataloging purposes (keyword searches).
- Exporting information from a scanned drawing to a word processing, spreadsheet, or database application.

Key Points About Converting Text

- The text conversion tools are optimized for images with a resolution of 300 dpi.
- Text conversion tools only work with binary images.
- For text changes to the location or rotation angle rather than to the content, use the Raster Entity Manipulation tools.

Converted text displays in a verification dialog box. The verification process is very important because no OCR engine is 100 percent accurate. Although text that does not match the current dictionary is highlighted in the edit pane, it is recommended that you review all of the text for accuracy. Part numbers, quantities, and sizing information critical to many construction documents might not be highlighted by the spelling checker.

All of the standard text-editing practices are supported by the edit pane, including basic formatting, search and replace tools, and hard copy output.

Working with Optical Character Recognition

Procedure: Setting Up a Drawing for Text Conversion

Before selecting one of the text recognition tools, use the following steps to set up your drawing:

1. Insert the image containing the text to be converted and verify that the color depth and resolution are correct.

2. Set a text style for the new text.

3. Set a layer for the new text.

4. In the Raster Tools tab, in the Vectorize & Recognize Text panel, expand the OCR flyout and click Recognize Text.

5. Select a language for the text to be recognized and for the spell checker.

6. Use the AutoCAD style list to select the correct text style.

7. Verify that all of the other settings are correct. Click OK.

Text Conversion Considerations

It is recommended that you use the text recognition tools when large blocks of text are to be converted for use in other drawings or applications or for editing. It is rare that all of the text in a drawing would need to be converted.

Before you begin working with the text recognition tools, consider the following issues:

Consideration	Action
Which text needs to be converted?	Determine whether the content is going to change, the text is going to be used outside the current drawing, or the text is going to be reused repeatedly.
Is the current image bitonal?	Use Change Color Depth to set the type to Bitonal.
What is the current resolution?	Use Change Density to set the resolution to 300 dpi.
What should the resulting text look like?	Set an AutoCAD text style and layer.
Does the text have a regular appearance?	Use Recognize Setup to work with machine- or hand-printed text.

Exercise: Use Text Recognition

In this exercise, you will convert scanned text into standard AutoCAD text.

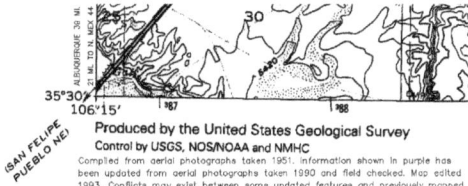

1. Open ...\Converting Text\TextRecog.dwg.

2. In the Raster Tools tab, in the Vectorize & Recognize Text panel, expand the OCR flyout and click Optical Character Recognition (OCR) Setup.

3. In the Text Recognition Setup dialog box, do the following:

   - Under Input, in Selection Shape, click Polygonal.
   - In the AutoCAD style list, verify that title is selected.

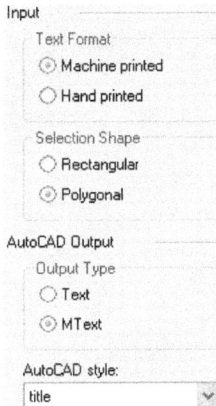

4. Under Removal Method, do the following, if not already selected:

   - Click Rub.
   - Select Enable verifier.

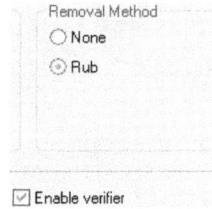

5. Click OK.

6. In the Raster Tools tab, in the Vectorize & Recognize Text panel, expand the OCR flyout and click Recognize Text.

7. At the prompt, pick 4 points to define a box around most of the notes. Press ENTER.

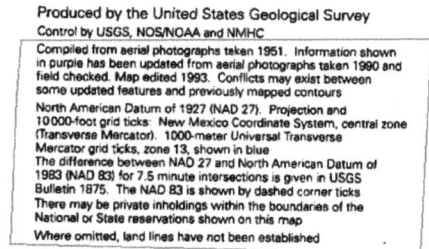

8. In the Verify Text dialog box, you can use the View controls to display the text in the Edit window at the bottom of the Verify Text dialog box more clearly.

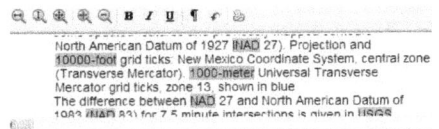

Uncertain words are highlighted in green, rejected characters are highlighted in yellow, and unrecognized characters display as red tiles.

9. Click any uncertain areas to correct the recognized text. For example, (NAD 27) has been recognized as INAD 27).

10. When done, click OK. Press ESC to complete the command.

11. In the Raster Tools tab, in the Vectorize & Recognize Text panel, expand the OCR flyout and click Recognize Text.

12. Enter **A** to set the text angle. Enter **90**. Press ENTER.

13. Draw a polygon around the text beginning with Albuquerque, as shown in the following illustration.

14. In the dialog box, correct any errors. Click OK. Press ESC to complete the command.

Chapter Summary

Having completed this chapter, you can:

- Use vectorization tools for interactive conversion.
- Use vectorization line-following tools.
- Create contours using the Contour Follower.
- Convert text.

www.ingramcontent.com/pod-product-compliance
Lightning Source LLC
Chambersburg PA
CBHW081524220326
41598CB00036B/6323